Flourishing on the Edge of Faith

Seven Practices for a New We

Andrew DeCort, PhD

BitterSweet Collective
Washington, D.C.
2022

Praise for *Flourishing on the Edge of Faith*

"This book is at once comforting and discomfiting in a deeply personal way. I confront the devastation of war every day, and so I keep a poster on my office wall that reminds me, 'Don't be ashamed to stand for peace.' Whether you're a believer or not, *Flourishing on the Edge of Faith* will give you the shameless courage necessary to stand for peace."

Dr. Alex de Waal
Executive Director, World Peace Foundation

———

"This book is subtle and radical. Its stated aim is modest: to introduce you to a practice of prayer. But if you open your heart enough, it will introduce you to a new worldview, and maybe even change your world. Prayer is powerful. Faith is powerful. This book will show you the way."

Eboo Patel
Founder and President, Interfaith America

———

"*Flourishing on the Edge of Faith* is pitched as speaking to 'those on the edges of faith,' but its fresh, blazing, Jesus-intoxicated spiritual vision can speak to everyone. What looks at first like an exposition of the Lord's Prayer turns out to be a powerful, honest, high-intensity, high-integrity invitation to know Jesus and practice his way. For me, it was like being introduced to Jesus again. I love this book! I think Andrew is one of the most inspired, and inspiring, Christian thinkers and practitioners that I know anywhere in the world."

Rev. Dr. David Gushee
Past President, The American Academy of Religion and The Society of Christian Ethics

———

"I am an atheist, would never dream of praying, and believe that religion has wrought much evil in the world. I also think that religion can be a powerful ally in the quest for truth, justice, and human fulfillment. In its clarity, compassion, and expansive spirit, *Flourishing on the Edge of Faith* embodies the kind of Christianity that I do not hesitate to get behind."

David Livingstone Smith
Author of *On Inhumanity: Dehumanization and How to Resist It*

———

"In this passionate call to theological engagement, Andrew DeCort has presented the Lord's Prayer as a 'life practice'—whose embodiment is nothing less than an opportunity to incarnate love and moral responsibility in our world. *Flourishing on the Edge of Faith* is a guidebook for the soul."

Professor Michael Fishbane
Nathan Cummings Distinguished Service Professor of Jewish Studies Emeritus, University of Chicago

———

"*Flourishing on the Edge of Faith* is a powerful reflection on the Lord's Prayer, written with sensitivity and sophistication. Andrew DeCort loves Jesus; he is on a journey of discovery and longs for others to live lives of 'fierce flourishing.' *Flourishing on the Edge of Faith* is engaging, transparent and practical, filled with powerful stories, written by a man whose faith has taken him from the University of Chicago to Ethiopia's devastating civil war. Through it all prayer has sustained Andrew; his hope, in the form of this book, is for prayer to sustain us as well."

Peter Wehner
Writer for *The New York Times* and *The Atlantic*, author of *The Death of Politics: How to Heal Our Frayed Republic After Trump*

———

"In *Flourishing on the Edge of Faith*, DeCort offers a fresh, invigorating reinterpretation of a prayer so familiar that even those of us outside the Christian faith can recite it from memory. He does so through a fascinating blend of spiritual teaching, theology, history and memoir, rich in insight and brimming with passion. Much of what DeCort writes is intensely personal, stemming from his years in Ethiopia during its slide into civil war, a period in which he was himself subject to hate speech and death threats. The result is a book from which even those who are not religious can draw courage and inspiration."

Tom Gardner
East Africa Correspondent, *The Economist*

"Andrew makes the spirituality of Jesus accessible as he demystifies and strips away the religious trauma of American spirituality, inviting us into the practice of nonviolence formed by prayer. He communicates the revolutionary prayer of Jesus that has echoed throughout history, giving us a fresh perspective on what it means to be human, and reflects through the lens of Jesus' prayer on a better way forward than violence, a way that can actually save us from pain, conflict and death. Andrew's compelling writing paints a picture of what human flourishing can look like during an age of worry and violence."

David Gungor
Singer-Songwriter, The Brilliance

"There is a field beyond belief and disbelief; Andrew DeCort guides us there. *Flourishing on the Edge of Faith* is a practical rumination unlike any other. Andrew meets so many of us where we are: disenchanted with and disaffected by co-opted, corrupted, and weaponized faiths. But he reorients us to that inner spark—our deepest desires for connection with the transcendent and for a world today in which goodness can finally prevail. And he gives us the tools to deepen our journey, or to begin it anew, with fresh energy and spirit. *Flourishing on the Edge of Faith* is pure magic."

Gregory Khalil
Co-Founder and President, Telos Group

———

"This book is truly wonderful and transforming for me in praying the Lord's Prayer or Our Father! Although this prayer is well-known, there are few who can say why Jesus asks us to pray these words, or how doing so could lead to flourishing. To see what is so familiar anew, to move from the vague sense of significance into a deeper understanding, to unpack the heart of Jesus's teaching in those seven lines, are gifts of tremendous worth. Andrew DeCort has given us a rare treasure in *Flourishing on the Edge of Faith*, transforming that which so often becomes rote into a tool for renewal."

Sarah Borden Sharkey
Professor of Philosophy, Wheaton College

———

"Follow DeCort as words as simple as 'Our' or as strange as 'Hallowed' become gateways for us to follow Jesus's most disturbing teaching— to love our enemies. You'll undergo a fierce change of heart and a revolution of the mind. I can't praise DeCort's accomplishments enough. The door you've shut against God's abiding love for you will fall open for good."

Suzanne Ross
Founder of unRival Network

———

"I experienced something radical while reading this book and 'bathing' in my belovedness: peace, security, surprise, calmness, stillness, an odd euphoria. I've heard the exhortation for literally decades, but I'd never felt it before. Andrew's writing was what made that practice accessible to me."

Recovering drug addict

"For those like me who have all but thrown in the towel on Christianity, this is an inspiring and fresh look at what it really means to follow Jesus. Rigorous yet accessible throughout, DeCort draws upon diverse artists, thinkers, and doers to challenge us to a more spacious, grounded, and other-centered life of faith."

David Ellis
Co-Founder and Director, Flow Equity

"I think of Dr. Andrew DeCort as the C.S. Lewis or Dietrich Bonhoeffer of our time. His writing provides rare and breathtaking insight into the words of Jesus and shows how they have the power to help us reimagine every moment of our lives."

Grant Hensel
Founder, The RoundUp App

"*Flourishing on the Edge of Faith* sings a protest song of radical belonging, unconditional love, and miraculous newness. Reading it had my heart racing and eyes watering. It reverberates with the messy and profound goodness of being human together."

Jenna Heath
M.D., Obstetrician-Gynecologist,
University of Southern California Keck School of Medicine

"People today are not only uninterested in the Christian faith but antagonistic to it. Andrew weaves stories and current events into this book that not only keep our interest but are highly practical and relevant in helping readers re-engage with faith in Jesus. I highly recommend this book for people working to love the world."

Dr. Wayne Gordon
Pastor, Lawndale Community Church; President Emeritus,
Christian Community Development Association

———

"*Flourishing on the Edge of Faith* is a beautifully robust book that seeks to transform us to the core. If your inner critic is strong and your spiritual life feels stymied, let this book revoice you into the way of flourishing."

Jay Stringer
Psychotherapist and author of *Unwanted:
How Sexual Brokenness Reveals Our Way to Healing*

———

"Fiercely attentive to 'the undying ache of the universe,' *Flourishing on the Edge of Faith* will become a crucial guide for people who long for the world to be what it should be, and someday will be."

Steven Garber
Author of *The Seamless Life: A Tapestry of Love and
Learning, Worship and Work*

———

"This is a book for all who seek to learn from Jesus. I will return to it again and again."

George Kalantzis
Professor of Theology at Wheaton College and
Senior Fellow of the International Association for Refugees

———

ISBN 978-1-958865-00-2

For Jane, who birthed me in divine belovedness
and taught me to pray with Jesus.

For Graham, who first believed in my writing
and invested many years ago.

For Dave, my pastor in exile:
"You've got books inside of you."

For Joelle, Mark, Jenna, and Ty:
our cherished eucatastrophe.

For Lily:
my lover, teacher, painter, and Patronus.

Seeing your face is like seeing the face of God

"It's the age of doubt
And I doubt we'll figure it out
Is it you or is it me?
The age of anxiety

It's a maze of mirrors
It's a hologram of a ghost
And you can't quite touch it
Which is how it hurts us the most

So we keep it all inside
And hide it deep in a drawer
Say your prayers tonight
Someone finds it after the war"

Arcade Fire

The epigraph above is from Arcade Fire, "Age of Anxiety I,"
track 1 on WE (Columbia Records, 2022).

Contents

Preface

Flourishing on the Edge of Faith

> *"How do you know that you're right, if you're
> not nervous anymore?"*
> **The Killers**[1]

I wrote this book for people on the edge of faith who are seeking a flourishing life. Three of my friends' faces frequently came to my mind as I wrote, and I want to briefly introduce them to you.[2]

On a brisk November afternoon in Chicago's Humboldt Park, Hannah and I met up at a Puerto Rican cafe. The golden beauty of autumn was giving way to the bleak gray of winter. We got some hot chocolate to stay warm and set out on a walk through the park's urban prairie.

From the start, Hannah admitted that meeting with me—a former professor and spiritual mentor—was difficult. She was tired of Christian friends expressing their "concern" for her and trying to win her back. Soon enough, she indignantly exclaimed, "F*ck Christianity!"

Hannah's uncensored anger didn't offend me. In fact, it struck me as a fierce testimony of just how much faith mattered to her and how disappointed she was with the community that once defined her. Hannah is a champion of others and a relentlessly thoughtful human being. Christian hypocrisy, tribal boundaries, and indifference to "others"—refugees, gay people, the urban poor in the community where she teaches—had pushed her away. She needed to keep seeking for something more through the winter of her faith.

Soon after, I talked over WhatsApp with my friend Isabell in Germany. Her smile lights her face with warmth, and her voice carries a mirthful kindness. Even so, Isabell lives with an incurable illness that causes her chronic pain as she trains to become a pastor.

Our conversations often circle around vulnerability, loss, and doubt. After growing up in a charismatic church, Isabell has often expressed an unsettling sense of God's absence. Tragedy in her family and scandals in the church have driven her to question if God is even there.

In this particular conversation, Isabell confessed, "I miss God." She said that this feeling was like "an ache and a drawing," like a painful emptiness mixed with deep hopefulness. She experiences it when she walks in nature or allows herself to slow down and rest.

Searching for the right English word, Isabell told me with her wonderful German accent that she feels like a *pioneer*. She's become a person who no longer walks the dualistic path of either being a Christian or having no faith at all. She disbelieves the cliche comfort that "everything happens for a reason" and emphasized, "Most of the time my pain just sucks." Still, she described a vision she saw of ashes turning into a garden and said, "Sometimes in small sacred moments, God gives me hope that I will be able to turn my pain into something that will help others flourish when they're not okay."

Awhile later, I talked with my friend Michael, who's originally from China but now living in California. Michael is funny, empathetic, and ambitious. He's a brilliant engineer working on cutting-edge technology for Apple.

After hearing about his achievements at work and weekends at Las Vegas, I asked Michael about his relationship with God. He answered, "I don't know." He wasn't brushing me off. This was his honest answer.

Michael went on to say that he's stopped going to church—like most of his Christian friends have—and that he pays less attention to his spiritual development. He still prays, but not as frequently. His job has been consuming, and faith has started to feel like a superficial "tag of belonging—like being white or Asian." Despite loving his groundbreaking work, Michael confessed his concern that we're drifting into spiritual emptiness—into a narcissistic culture of materialism, loneliness, and violence.

At the end of our call, Michael told me that he's looking for guidance and tangible goals. He wants to rediscover a flourishing life. But he said that he needs spiritual practices that can survive in a nonreligious environment.

This book is for people like my friends—people on the edge of faith. Their words are live wires in my heart and mind as I share this book with you:

F*ck Christianity.

I miss God.

I don't know.

They experience pain and anger and uncertainty and the rebellious ache for something more. They're imperfect and passionate people who courageously seek a fiercer flourishing for themselves and our world.

I'm one of these people.

I write this book out of my own experience of voluntary displacement from any traditional religious community. Similar to Isabell, I feel like a pioneer. I'm learning to seek God everywhere, in everyone, in relationships of love and justice for a fierce flourishing.

Wherever you are on the edge of faith, I offer this book to you with my gratitude, honesty, and hope. I've worked around the world as a pastor, professor, and peace practitioner in conflict zones. I'll tell some of these stories in the pages that follow. But mainly, I'm a fellow human being with my own burning questions, intimate pain, and unrelenting desire for flourishing in our shared universe.

Thank you for reading my book and joining me in this journey.

Preparation

The Spirituality of Jesus

*"I want to be free enough to live the questions of
the spiritual life without fearing the consequences."*
Henri Nouwen[1]

What Is This Book About?

Our Father in heaven,
Hallowed be Your name.
Your kingdom come, Your will be done, on earth as it is in heaven.
Give us today our daily bread
and forgive us our sins as we forgive others.
Don't lead us into temptation but deliver us from evil.
Yours is the kingdom and the power and the glory—forever.

This book is about those words, which are likely familiar to you.

They're an ancient prayer that Jesus of Nazareth taught to his students in the three years of his career as a wandering teacher. They've been recited in the morning chapels of parochial schools and in the Sunday services of ordered churches. But just as often, they've been prayed in situations of intense distress and danger as we'll see. They usually go by the name "The Lord's Prayer" or "The Our Father," but Jesus himself taught them without any such title.

More precisely, this book is about what those words teach us when we pray them. This seven-line prayer—which so many of us can repeat with unthinking reflex—reflects a profound spiritual vision that was the core of Jesus's life and work. This vision can be captured in one simple word: flourishing.

This book, then, is about learning to live lives of fierce flourishing by praying the words that Jesus taught to a wildly diverse crowd of people in ancient Palestine. As we'll see, Jesus wasn't stringing together random requests or pious petitions. He was subtly responding to primal questions that search to the heart of what it means to be human—then, now, and always. And in this way, Jesus was outlining an integrated spiritual practice for our mature human flourishing.

Why pray? Because when we pray with Jesus, we practice flourishing. That's this book in a nutshell.

I wrote it down amidst death threats and Ethiopia's devastating civil war, a story I'll tell in chapter six. This wasn't the intention of the countless people who promised to kill me, but they pushed me deeper into the primal power of Jesus's spiritual practice. This is a spirituality for all of us that offers hope to all of us. We are all *we*, children of our divine Parent, and I want to begin by blessing my enemy-siblings with the flourishing Jesus promises.

Who Was Jesus?

Jesus has a provocative and gripping biography. He was a soul on fire.[2]

Jesus was born to impoverished parents named Mary and Joseph in Bethlehem under the dark shadow of Rome's violent empire. Before his birth, his young mother sang a protest song about how her son would turn things upside down, bringing good news to the poor and powerless. Soon after, an old man named Simeon held the newborn in his arms and said that Jesus was destined to "cause the rising and falling" of many in his society. Jesus would become a *contradiction*—"a sign that would be spoken against."

The upheaval that Mary and Simeon foresaw erupted rapidly and ruthlessly in Jesus's story. As a child, Jesus narrowly escaped an atrocious political massacre ordered by the local tyrant Herod. Jesus's desperate family fled to neighboring Egypt, and his earliest memories were likely filled with being a vulnerable refugee far from home.

After Herod's death, Jesus resettled to restive Nazareth. A rural village in northern Israel, Nazareth was synonymous with marginality. There Jesus was trained as a carpenter and developed in obscurity as he learned his craft. Jesus's vocational formation is significant. The elegant simplicity and precise beauty of his craftsmanship is carved into the short prayer that he would design.

But Mary got her son right. Around the age of thirty—still a youth in most cultures—Jesus launched a public movement. It all began at the Jordan River when Jesus had an engulfing experience of his divine belovedness. As he's ritually bathed in the river by his radical cousin John, Jesus sees heaven open and hears God say, "You are my beloved child; I delight in you." This unconditional divine affirmation became the womb of Jesus's revolutionary movement.

John was soon arrested by Herod's son for his very public critiques of corrupt political power. Herod Junior went on to cut off John's head in exchange for a lap dance. But immediately after John's arrest, Jesus daringly went public and made John's message his own. He declared, *Change how you think; the kingdom of heaven is so close.*

Jesus then started traveling, teaching in public places, and healing people all throughout Palestine. Sometimes he invited other youth to follow him and join the movement. Other times, Jesus met people in pain and encouraged them to return home to share with others the healing they had experienced.

From the start, Jesus shared meals with public enemies and sex-workers. This controversial practice got him infamously branded "the friend of sinners." But Jesus saw these inclusive parties as foretastes of the in-breaking kingdom of heaven that he announced. He protected women from men's deadly violence and welcomed them into his community. In fact, Jesus's movement was funded by a collective of women—including dissident women inside Herod's household.

Jesus premiered his public teaching in the most unlikely way. To a wildly diverse crowd of people under Rome's imperial occupation, he proclaimed God's sacred happiness. The poor, the grieving, and the persecuted—he called them *blessed.*

Then Jesus taught these people to pray together to *our* Father, inviting them into a new *we* that was unimaginable in the embattled identities of his society. Jesus concluded his teaching by claiming that we meet God whenever we meet people who are hungry, thirsty, naked, foreign, diseased, and incarcerated. According to Jesus, this revaluation of the oppressed and unwanted is where history is going in the end, when heaven comes to earth.

Throughout his teaching, Jesus told scandalous stories that inspired people to reimagine God, how they saw others, and the meaning of life. For example, his Parable of the Good Samaritan celebrated the most hated person in his society as a moral hero who shows us the way to heaven. Samaritans were the ultimate ethnic others, religious heretics, and political enemies in Jewish culture. But Jesus lifts up a Samaritan, who crossed cultural boundaries to embrace a victim of violence, as the paradigm for how to live forever.

Jesus's story was essentially like a preacher today making their signature sermon about the *good* gay person or the *good* Muslim or the *good* illegal immigrant. Jesus did just that by making a Samaritan the hero of his story. This was the radioactive energy behind Jesus's most unprecedented teaching: *Love your enemies*.

Unsurprisingly, then, Jesus routinely broke the rules to include others. He praised foreigners for their faith. He embraced the demonized and reintegrated splintered people with themselves and their communities. He called out the rich and famous, the religious and powerful at home in the belittling boxes of us versus them.

Jesus's life was intense from the start, and he embodied a profound emotional honesty. His tears flowed freely for the dying and endangered, for women and children in war zones. Jesus wept.

Jesus even went into the epicenter of his world, the Temple in Jerusalem. Rather than paying his respects, Jesus overturned the tables of those who had turned God into business. Outside the Temple, he offered new beginnings to the spiritually bankrupt.

Predictably, then, death threats dog Jesus's story from the outset. When you love the enemy, you become the enemy. The cultural guardians and religious gatekeepers found him to be too unreligious, too countercultural and threatening to the status quo to stomach.

Jesus shattered their entrenched expectations for a nationalistic messiah who would restore Israel's greatness.

After three short years, Jesus had become *truly* intolerable. And so he was arrested just outside Jerusalem by an armed militia on charges of "subverting the nation." After a mock trial before a kangaroo court, Jesus was condemned as a public enemy. He was brutally tortured and executed with Rome's excruciating weapon of death: the cross. Alas, this violent lynching remains all-too-familiar to us to this day.[3]

Still, Jesus himself had a different interpretation of his death. This is why Jesus defiantly appropriated the Roman cross as the emblem of his movement, subverting a symbol of torture into a sign of self-giving love. And so Jesus died in the most defiantly beautiful way, unlike anyone before him in history, as we'll see.

Three days later, his previously crestfallen followers started rebelliously filling Jerusalem with news that Jesus was alive. They said that God had raised Jesus from the dead, forever beyond the vice grip of human domination. What looked like a tragic end was really the embodiment of an infinitely buoyant love.

Their daring message was clear: Jesus wasn't a misguided malcontent on a suicide mission or a mere martyr. He incarnated the undying ache at the heart of the universe.[4]

Soon after, the resurrected Jesus handed his movement off to his ragtag band of students, the practitioners of his craft. He told them that his way of life is for everyone everywhere. And so he sent them out, across all the borders of the empire, to do what he did: to invite people to be baptized in divine love and to practice this unkillable way of flourishing. Jesus called it good news for a cold-hearted world.

And against all odds, Jesus—the massacre survivor, the countercultural teacher and friend of sinners, the executed criminal—had just launched what would become the most successful social movement in history. The empire denounced his followers as "atheists" for defiantly disbelieving in the violent gods that justified its oppression. But these gritty women and men gave their lives for their new atheism. And their heretical good news inspired the world to believe like never before.

For the last two thousand years, billions of people across diverse cultures and distant continents have experienced Jesus as this singular fusion of divine and human life—as the face of God with us and for our flourishing. Hannah Arendt, a major 20th century political theorist and herself a secular Jew, saw who Jesus was. In her book *On Revolution*, she called Jesus "the only completely valid, completely convincing" embodiment of goodness in history.[5]

So this book is about that revolutionary person's prayer. I believe Jesus's prayer encapsulates his entire spirituality and shows us how to practice a fierce flourishing still today. Two millennia in, we're only just beginning to discover the profound implications of who we can become when we pray with Jesus.

What Is Prayer?

I'll be honest: prayer wasn't my thing growing up. I struggled for years to grasp why it really matters, and it wasn't a consistent part of my life. Maybe you're like me, and you've given up on prayer or never really tried it.

But with Jesus, I've discovered that prayer isn't pious and impotent, a private act or religious performance detached from the rest of our lives and world. It's become the oxygen of my humanity, and I want everyone to experience this. It comes alive when we learn to pray with Jesus.

So what is prayer?

Prayer is the simple, courageous, creative act of patiently opening our entire being to God. It's an open posture of attention, welcome, and expectation for the transcendence of heaven in our embodied experience. This kind of vulnerable, listening presence transforms who we are and how we live with others. Its silence and stillness can profoundly center, heal, and enliven our humanity.[6]

The practice of praying with Jesus, then, is about what we do with our most precious resource—our attention.[7] The psychiatrist Curt Thompson writes, "Ultimately we become what we pay attention to."[8] Prayer animates our imagination and desire, our decisions and action in the world as one interconnected flow. From this perspective, prayer is among our most practical activities and has tremendous power to orient and energize our work, culture, and politics—if we don't derail and fall for the egocentric, tribalistic counterfeits.

I see prayer as premeditation for practice, an idea I'll return to in chapter six. It doesn't always work in the ways we want or expect— certainly not like a device that automatically answers our dictates on demand. That's a modernization of ancient magical thinking. Prayer works, but it primarily *works on us*.

So prayer is spiritual practice that sculpts our consciousness, character, and community as we converse with God and invite God's sacred Presence into every corner of our lives. This includes our most painful and distressing experiences.[9] Here I'm reminded of the poet Amanda Gorman's sharp line: "We prayed for a miracle. / What we got was a mirror."[10] With patient practice, the prayer of Jesus becomes a mirror in which to see and be transformed with God and others for our shared flourishing.

Brother Lawrence was a 17th century French mystic and author of the spiritual classic *The Practice of the Presence of God*. Lawrence described prayer as an ongoing conversation with God that changes our lives. This has been one of the most seminal insights and experiences of my life once I started taking prayer seriously.

Prayer is talking with God. It's something we can do anywhere, at any time, with anyone. Lawrence described how cleaning the kitchen and repairing shoes became some of his most meaningful times of prayer.[11] I experience this while taking walks, talking with friends, and doing daily work like washing the dishes. The prayer of Jesus is perfect for this kind of ongoing conversation with God that defies our deadening sacred-secular dualism.[12]

Praying with Jesus, then, is a form of mindfulness that orients, energizes, and integrates all of our other worthwhile words and work in the world. It flows in and out of our embodied desires, decisions, and capacities.[13] As Martin Luther King Jr. reminds us, and Jesus made clear, prayer is never a *substitute* for action. But it's the essential *source* for action that's wise and beautiful and enduring.[14] Prayer is a practice of freedom, a resistance movement of willfully reclaiming our attention, imagination, and desire from what would otherwise distract, conform, and consume us.

As we talk with the God who called Jesus beloved, what we love, who we are, and how we live are being healed and transformed within a wider horizon of radical hope. And so prayer becomes a birthplace of change that starts rippling out into the world as we practice becoming new kinds of prayerful, flourishing creatures.

What Is Practice?

Before moving on, I want to briefly illustrate what I mean when I call prayer *practice*.

When I was a boy, I loved playing basketball, whether in the blazing heat of summer or the bitter cold of winter. My dad noticed this love and generously laid a slab of cement in our tiny backyard so I could play every day. If you've seen the documentary *The Last Dance* about the 1990s Chicago Bulls, that was my childhood dream.

But I was an entirely one-sided player. Despite my love for the game, I only ever played to my natural right-handed strengths. My left hand remained attached to my body but unpracticed and basically useless. And this made me easy to guard, because I could only dribble and drive to my right.

So one gray day, my discontent drove me to make a choice that changed my game. I went out to that cement slab in the dead of winter and spent several hours shooting a thousand shots, one after another—exclusively with my left, semi-frozen hand.

Unsurprisingly, the initial results were dismal and disappointing. My skinny left arm was barely strong enough to heave the ball up to the hoop. And it was far too wobbly to aim with any accuracy. Simply catapulting the ball close to where I wanted it was challenging and mostly unsuccessful.

When we practice, we encounter this paradox: distress is the sign that our practice has truly begun. And when we don't give up, it powerfully strengthens our flourishing. But it rarely feels like this in the beginning. In fact, the distress of practice often makes us feel like we're wasting our time or wasting away. And so we easily retreat to more comfortable habits that soothe our distress.[15]

Noticing and practicing *through* this paradox is essential for our flourishing to become mature and creative. It's why Jesus said that we should "pray and not give up."

Thankfully, I kept at it on the court. And after a few hundred shots, I became conscious of this paradoxical experience unfolding in my body: I was getting exhausted—*and stronger*. My left hand didn't feel quite so unfamiliar or foreign to me anymore. I was starting to be able to actually *shoot* the ball.

As night fell, I was drained after my thousandth shot. But I was also energized like never before. I was starting to play basketball as a full-bodied player. I had a new sense of control and creativity. After several weeks of continuing this practice, I could dribble, drive, and shoot with my left hand almost as well as I could with my right. What was previously impossible became possible for me, even if my last dance wasn't to be in the NBA.

A simple distinction may be helpful before we start practicing prayer with Jesus. I'll return to it often throughout this book. *Habit* is what we repetitively do, whether we realize it or not, and whether it helps us or not. I was an exclusively right-handed player by *habit*. And habit fully grown often amounts to addiction or dependence on something that limits and ultimately harms us.[16]

But *practice* is what we repeatedly *choose* to do, whether we feel it or not. It's doing the same thing over and over again, with patient attention and courageous intentionality. Thompson writes, "Practice tends to make permanent."[17] When we practice through our disappointment and distress, it becomes part of our fully embodied personhood. Practice fully grown is flourishing.

And practice unlocks the previously impossible. With time and imperfection, we're empowered to do what we love with new fluency and freedom. In the game of this book, we learn to be human like the radical Jesus I briefly introduced above. We flourish.

What Is Flourishing?

I realize that the word "flourishing" may sound flimsy to some of us. But it traces back to *flowering* and suggests the organic integration of fragile vulnerability and mature beauty—of self-revealing weakness and resilient strength.[18]

By flourishing, I mean a life that is growing in being more fully alive. It's deeply rooted, increasingly open, and courageously energized with a radical love that can endure through our most distressing experiences of pain, conflict, and death.[19]

Jesus describes this kind of flourishing as something that's ultimately undying and everlasting. Its roots reach back to the origins of our universe, and its life stretches forward into our future beyond death. It starts here and now, on earth with others, in our daily lives and vocations.

This flourishing is fiercer than the commercialized offerings that only focus on happiness, health, wealth, and winning. These popular options can be addictive, because they suppress our painful experiences of insecurity, conflict, loss, and death. But they're ultimately dishonest and inevitably crumble under the weight of reality.

What invests Jesus's practice of flourishing with enduring credibility for me is its honesty. It begins in our divine belovedness, but it's ruggedly real about our suffering. It resists what Dr. King called our addiction to "easy answers and half-baked solutions," and it invites us to embrace the risk of what John Lewis called "good trouble."[20] When we practice Jesus's prayer, it becomes a soul-body-world reintegrating spirituality that simultaneously tears, heals, and strengthens the vital muscles of our humanity.

With Jesus, then, we learn to practice prayer through this paradox: Our fiercest flourishing comes alive when we wrestle with our distress, face our darkest drives, and learn to trustingly hold on and let go when everything feels like it's falling apart.

This counter-intuitive wisdom has been attested to by many of our most credible spiritual guides throughout history. For example, Dietrich Bonhoeffer, the rugged Nazi-resister, wrote soon before the Gestapo arrested him, "Personal suffering is a more useful key, a more fruitful principle than personal happiness for exploring the meaning of the world in contemplation and action." With his last words hours before his execution, Bonhoeffer defiantly proclaimed, "This is for me the end, but also the beginning... Our victory is certain."[21]

With patient practice, Jesus's flourishing is woven into the cellular tissue of our lives and world. It becomes the breath and bone of our very being in our universe. Our questions and confidence, weakness and strength, vulnerability and resilience, grief and hope are reintegrated. The horizons of our humanity expand—stretching back to our beginning in divine belovedness, journeying through the painful complexity of our history, and reaching forward into a future of ultimate belonging in which we all finally come home.[22]

Where Is This Book Going?

The rest of this book unfolds in seven chapters. Each chapter explores one line from Jesus's prayer and the core question that he seeks to answer through it. I want to offer an aerial overview of where we're going, so the integrated progression of Jesus's seven spiritual practices is centered and clear from the start.

Each movement of Jesus's prayer is carefully crafted and tightly connected to the next. This isn't a series of random requests but an integrated journey into full human flourishing. Each practice takes us one step forward, and the climax of our journey is found at the end, which brilliantly brings us back to our beginning.

We might think of this prayer as an elliptical movement progressing from our childhood, into adulthood, and looping back to a new childhood. It's the sacred passage from birth to death into rebirth.[23]

Chapter 1: Our Parent

Jesus starts with the primal question *Who is God?* The beginning is always here—in our divine belovedness. Jesus invites us to talk to God as our Parent who intimately knows us, infinitely loves us, and eternally cares for us as God's children. This river of love gives us life, heals our painful insecurity, and washes away our prideful superiority to others. In prayer, we learn to speak the language of God's new *we*. Divine belovedness is our birthplace and destiny.

But stopping here all too easily drifts into a false familiarity with God. It ultimately turns "God" into a coping mechanism for ourselves and a weapon against others. There is more to practice.

Chapter 2: Hallowed Be Your Name

So Jesus turns immediately to ask *How should we talk about God?* Jesus invites us to hallow God's name with radical reverence. This practice reveals that we can't properly say God's name or grasp who God is. Holy Mystery strips us of certainty and exposes us to God's transcendent otherness beyond all human knowledge or power. Paradoxically, we find *God* afresh by losing "God."

But stopping here easily gets stuck in deconstruction. This is an essential step but not the whole journey. We need to keep moving, lest we get stranded in a purely critical and passive spirituality. There is more to practice.

Chapter 3: Your Kingdom Come

So Jesus next asks us *What do you want?* Here Jesus opens our imagination and ignites our desire by inviting us to pray for God's kingdom to come on earth. This is God's dream for our world, and Jesus describes it with five prophetic signs: countercultural love, mutual relationships, integrated healing, nonviolent witness against injustice, and everyday action. I'll unpack each one in chapter three. As we pray with Jesus, our dreams and desires find orientation and energy for what is truly important and enduring, our cosmic endgame in the kingdom of heaven.

But stopping here easily inflates into an overlofty spirituality. Humans are addicted to messiah complexes, and this arrogant ambition always suppresses our basic needs and the empathy required for our embodied vulnerability. There is more to practice.

Chapter 4: Give Us Our Daily Bread

So in the fourth, fulcrum movement of his prayer, Jesus asks us *How much is enough?* Here we begin integrating Jesus's previous three movements. God calls us beloved children and cares for our most basic needs. But God is mysterious and doesn't promise us surplus or invulnerable security. We're invited into a subversively simple vision of enough that centers on our daily bread with others. This practice calls us to a shared table of trust, interdependence, and empathy against consumeristic indifference and excess.

But reclining here easily drifts off into a dreamy denial of a troubling but essential recognition: We hurt each other and often can't even sit at the same table. These painful conflicts drive us apart and cast doubt on whether a shared flourishing is really possible. There is more to practice.

Chapter 5: Forgive Us as We Forgive Others

So in the second half of his prayer, Jesus calls us into spiritual adulthood and asks the sobering question *How do we begin again?* Here Jesus invites us to ask God to forgive us as we forgive others. We discover that forgiveness is the liberating power of new beginning. This practice honestly admits that we make mistakes, hurt each other, and need to start over by courageously holding on to people and releasing pain. It interrupts shame, resentment, and revenge. It depolarizes us and unlocks seemingly impossible futures of hope.[24]

But as Jesus's own biography illustrates, practicing this kind of prayerful life is disruptive to the status quo and will not go unopposed. And stopping with forgiveness may not dig deep enough into the roots of why we have conflict to begin with and so fail to prevent the painful cycle of conflict from escalating. There is more to practice.

Chapter 6: Don't Lead Us into Temptation but Deliver Us from Evil

So the penultimate question that Jesus poses to us is *Can violence save us?* Here we face head-on our addiction to seeking security in hardening ourselves, losing consciousness, and mirroring aggression in high-stress situations. In this distress, our divine belovedness often feels like a forgotten memory, and the chaos of evil is easily unleashed. So before conflict even begins, Jesus teaches us to premeditate peace by being fully present, verbally processing our distress with others, and centering our trust in God's promised deliverance. This radical nonviolence is nearly the peak of our flourishing.

But even here, in this mature place of our spiritual journey, we may still secretly harbor the illusion that our flourishing is ultimately about winning power and prestige for ourselves. Many of us do to the end. So there is still more to practice.

Chapter 7: Yours Is the Kingdom and the Power and the Glory—Forever

The final question that Jesus asks us is perhaps the most challenging of all: *Can you let go of power and prestige?* Here at last, Jesus invites us to defiantly divest our empires and to confess that all power and prestige are Yours—our Father's. This prayer leads us to the place where we accept death and learn to celebrate that life isn't about control and clout. The climax of our flourishing is letting go of these addictive drives and surrendering to God in radical trust. And this apparent loss safely takes us back to our beginning—to our divine belovedness where all of us are fully at home forever.

Our destiny returns to our origin but now with a mature history of flourishing emancipated from the power of death for everlasting life.

And *this* is everything.

What's at Stake?

"Ultimately we become what we pay attention to... Practice tends to make permanent," writes Curt Thompson. And prayer is primarily about what we do with our attention. So there's a lot at stake in whether we choose to practice prayer and, if so, what we choose to pray about.

Jesus carefully crafted his prayer. And we see that the beautiful grain of his spirituality is carved in the knotted tensions of our human experience. We bathe in our divine belovedness but tremble with radical reverence before holy Mystery. We passionately participate in God's dream for the earth but also break the bread of our embodied vulnerability. We courageously practice forgiveness but honestly face the roots of our aggression. We learn to let go but still hold on with unkillable hope.

This is what Jesus's prayer centers in our attention. When we practice it, this prayer cultivates a fierce flourishing, unshackled from immaturity and the addictions of our distress. It enlivens and enlarges our humanity, promising us radical hope in this life and beyond into the next steps of our transmortal journey. Like every sacred passage, Jesus's spiritual practice leads us into the unknown, while anchoring us securely in our unconditional divine belovedness.

According to Jesus, this spiritual practice is our life's work. It's the movement that integrates our flourishing and that requires our entire lives to fulfill. It's everything Jesus thinks we need to walk through life and the door of death without fear—forever.

At the end of his teaching, Jesus names what's at stake. He says, "Everyone who hears these words of mine and *practices* them is like a wise person who builds their house on the rock." But Jesus warns that without this practice, our lives will easily wash away in the seething storms of existence.[25]

The fierce flourishing that Jesus promises us has been my experience for the last twenty years of practicing with him through every stage of my journey. Some of them have been marked by exhilarating growth, deeply meaningful relationships, radical joy, professional success, and passionate work as a pastor, professor, and peace practitioner in conflict zones. Some of them have been mutilated with gnawing loneliness, the near-death of my marriage, repeated loss and suicidal grief, crushing burnout, terrifying death threats, and seemingly unbearable pain. I'll share some of these stories in the chapters ahead.

But through it all, I've found that Jesus's promise is trustworthy and stands the test of time. His spiritual practice can sustain and strengthen our flourishing in every season of our lives, including the wintry ones in which flourishing seems dead and hope haunts us like an inaccessible memory or impossible dream.

Like we saw in the Preface, perhaps you start this journey with Hannah saying "F*ck Christianity!" Or maybe you miss God like Isabell. Or maybe like Michael, you simply don't know.

Wherever you are on the edge of faith, I hope this book enlarges and energizes your flourishing for years to come. This is my prayer as we pray together with Jesus about our lives' crucial questions and primal possibilities.[26]

One last note before you dive in. My friends tell me that reading one subsection of this book per sitting—about three to five pages—has been a good rhythm for reading *Flourishing on the Edge of Faith*. Every reader has their own pace, but don't feel like you need to rush through an entire chapter at once.

Thank you again for sharing your attention, reading my book, and practicing flourishing with Jesus.

Who Is God?
Our Parent

A Practice of Divine Belovedness

> *"Nobody seems to love you enough."*
> **Lord Voldemort[1]**

> *"You must believe in the yes that comes back when you ask,
> 'Do you love me?' You must choose this yes even when
> you don't experience it."*
> **Henri Nouwen[2]**

Humanity's Ultimate Question

Jesus begins his prayer in the most primal place. He asks humanity's original and ultimate question: *Who is God?*

For Jesus and perhaps for all of us, the question of God is not academic or even religious. It searches to the heart of our humanity. Within it reverberates the intimate yet universal questions that define our search for meaning and value, for belonging and hope:

Where do we come from?
Are we loved?
Is everything going to be okay?
When we pray, is anyone listening?

The God we meet with Jesus is not an abstract idea to believe, a religious doctrine to defend, or a cultural identity marker to project. For Jesus, God is a personal Presence to address and encounter, even in our most vulnerable and painful experiences. Jesus invites us to call God our Father.

Of course, each of us has different and sometimes painful experiences of our human fathers.[3] My friend Ermias was a notorious gangster in Addis Ababa and was arrested over twenty times for his violence. I'll never forget him telling me the story of how he ripped off his enemy's ear and baked it into a cake. He then gave it to his mutilated enemy on his birthday as a bitter expression of contempt.

When Ermias started praying with Jesus, he instinctively called God our Mother, because his father was an abusive and absent man. But Ermias's mother was patiently present and unconditionally loving, even during the years of his violence when she couldn't be physically near him. She reminded Ermias of Jesus's God, and so Ermias talked to God as our Mother.

As Ermias prayed with Jesus, he grew into a beloved parent to many of Ethiopia's orphaned and abandoned street children. His anger and violence were transformed into a healing compassion that created a new family for the most unwanted.

As you read this chapter, like Ermias, I hope you feel free to read "Our Mother" or "Our Parent" where I write "Our Father." God is transgender, traced in all of our humanity but trapped in none of it.[4] My friend Isabell told me, "When I pray to God as Her, it opens so many new rooms in my soul and feelings of being at home." Perhaps this will also be your experience as you experiment in prayer.

For Jesus, a flourishing life begins in this primal place: acknowledging and embracing the presence of God our Father.

You Are My Beloved Child

Jesus's invitation to call God our Father is rooted in perhaps the most intimate, important moment of his own life—a moment that he invites us to share with him in prayer.

Before Jesus preaches a sermon or performs any public action, he journeys out into the wilderness. There he meets his radical cousin John by the river Jordan, where John is baptizing people from all over ancient Palestine.

This immersive water ritual was meant to symbolize new birth, a washing away of old ways of living and the start of a new way of being human with God. John called this *metanoia* in Greek or a revolutionized mind.

Jesus is plunged into the river by John and rises up with water washing over him. In this moment of sacred passage, he sees heaven open and hears the voice of God say to him, "You are my beloved son; I delight in you" (Matthew 3:17; Mark 1:11; Luke 3:22).

I suspect that many of us have had this heaven-opening experience at some point in our lives. We call it epiphany, insight, or enlightenment.

Its sacred message has been paraphrased in all sorts of ways. Hannah Arendt said, "I want you to be." Fred Rogers said, "I like you the way you are." The traditional Hindu greeting says, "I see God in you."

These heaven-opening words speak to the core of Jesus's identity. They engulf him in his divine belovedness. They express God's unconditional pleasure in his being and a secure attachment that bathes and enlivens Jesus's humanity like the river's water rushing around his body.

Our Father's primal declaration reveals that God understands our deeply human fear that we're ultimately alone and unwanted. From God's words, it also appears that Jesus knew this haunting inner pain. By this point in his life, Jesus had survived an atrocious political massacre, fled to a neighboring country as a child refugee, and grown up in a rural village synonymous with mockery. Jesus was woundedly familiar with loss, violence, and trauma as we've seen.[5]

Our primal fear of being unloved and abandoned sets in motion a desperate struggle to perform, prove, and project that we are worthy of love. It also often leads us into a numbed or self-mutilating existence with a cutting inner voice of insult, rejection, and aggression. Here we find the hidden roots of some of our most desperate addictions. I have battled with both tendencies of ambitious performance and self-loathing throughout my life. During my PhD studies at the University of Chicago, I often heard an inner voice whisper, "You're a piece of sh*t."

The timing, then, of God's heaven-opening message to Jesus is significant. Before Jesus has said or done anything that could seemingly earn love, God speaks this absolute affirmation into the core of his being: *You are my child; I love you; your existence brings me happiness*. It's unconditional.

And God doesn't just say this once at the beginning of Jesus's movement. God says it repeatedly. In fact, this is the singular message that we hear God revoice to Jesus throughout his life recorded in the Gospels. It's as if these words encompass everything our Father wants to say to us.

The second time comes at a crucial turning point when Jesus faces growing unpopularity and rejection. Like the first, Jesus steps away into solitude, this time up in the mountains. There he prays and hears our Father repeat, "You are my beloved son; I delight in you." Then, moments before Jesus's brutal execution and ultimate act of self-giving love, God echoes this soul-healing message yet again.[6]

I find it striking that even self-confessed atheists have had this experience of God. For example, Dinah Bazer was a 63-year-old grandmother and ovarian cancer survivor. She was paralyzed with fear that her cancer would return and consume her life. But after an innovative treatment organized by New York University, Dinah confessed:

> "I'm an atheist, I don't believe there is a God. But then I began to feel this love. Just overwhelming, all-encompassing love. And the way I describe it is being bathed in God's love, because I find no other way to describe it. I felt that I belonged, that I was part of everything and had the right to be here. How else do I describe it? Maybe what your mother's love felt like when you were a baby. This feeling of love was suffusing the entire experience."[7]

This atheist's experience of divine belovedness is uncannily like Jesus's baptism. She recalls being bathed and suffused with nurturing parental love. And this love washed away her fear of dying and embraced her with complete belonging.

My friend Simon Howard researches the testimonies of people who have had near-death experiences, and he's found a strikingly similar pattern. He told me,

> "I don't think I've listened to a single recounting of a near-death experience that hasn't included a profound sense of being overwhelmingly loved by a being that is identifiably

God, and that hasn't resulted in a new resolve for the experiencer to love others in their continued earthly life."[8]

This is who Jesus experienced God to be. God is the One who knows us, who loves us, and who delights in us. God declares this before we have said or done anything that could deserve love. And God continues declaring this to us even in the midst of fear, loss, and death. It's unconditional.

With his prayer's primal movement, then, Jesus invites us to talk to *this* God as *our* Father. He welcomes us to hear that divine whisper in the depths of our being. This Voice opens heaven and interrupts other gnawing voices of shame, performance, rejection, and aggression. *You are my beloved child; I delight in you. Nothing can make you less than that for me.* Henri Nouwen wrote that this divine belovedness "reveals the most intimate truth about all human beings, whether they belong to any particular tradition or not."[9]

This is where our practice of flourishing truly begins.

Love Your Enemies

This intimate, identity-healing experience of God as our loving Parent is the root of Jesus's unprecedented teaching. To this day, this teaching remains the most radical and hopeful social ethic in history: *Love your enemies* (Matthew 5:43-48; Luke 6:27-36).

These three words had never been put together in the same sentence before Jesus said them. The ancient world had abundant philosophies and religions that justified brutal revenge against enemies in the name of "God." At best, some encouraged non-retaliation as a spiteful expression of moral superiority or as a pragmatic survival strategy.[10] But no one had ever taught us to see the hated other as a beloved sibling in God's family. The ancient visions of God simply didn't support this radical love.

But Jesus boldly teaches us to love our enemies. He trains us to see their precious value and to desire their flourishing. And Jesus doesn't root this ethic in human reason, the desire for social change, pragmatic self-protection, or even the conversion of unbelievers. He roots it in God's character as our universal Father. *This* is how *God* loves.

With courageous originality, Jesus declares that God overflows with generosity to "the evil" and "the unjust." He describes God as "kind to the ungrateful and wicked." Jesus piles up incriminating epithets that would seemingly disqualify people from being worthy of basic rights or care, much less divine love. And then he insists that God loves even *them*, even if they don't love God back. God is the original enemy-lover (Matthew 5:45; Luke 6:35).

And this is God's perfection according to Jesus. What makes God *God* isn't raw power or the ability to bully people. God's *mercy* is God's Godness. It's God's desire to forgive, heal, and give good gifts that most essentially reveals real divinity. The family resemblance, then, that reveals God's children is their radical love even for their enemy siblings in God's sacred family (Luke 6:36; Matthew 5:48).

Jesus's baptism in divine belovedness led him to this unprecedented insight. Karin Sokel, a middle-aged life coach, had a similarly engulfing experience of her divine belovedness. And it led her to a strikingly similar place to where it led Jesus. She tells the award-winning researcher Michael Pollan,

> "I was in the presence of this absolute pure divine love and I was merging with it, in this explosion of energy... The core of our being, I now knew, is love. At the peak of the experience, I was literally holding the face of Osama bin Laden, looking into his eyes, feeling pure love from him and giving it to him. The core is not evil, it is love. I had the same experience with Hitler, and then someone from North Korea."[11]

The core of our being is love. This was Jesus's original insight, and

7

its radioactive energy inspired him to see even our most notorious enemies as ultimately beloved brothers and sisters in God's family.

If this strikes us as wishful thinking, Nelson Mandela is another rugged witness. He survived twenty-seven years of dehumanizing imprisonment under South Africa's brutal apartheid system. Still, Mandela insisted, "All [people], even the most seemingly cold-blooded, have a core of decency, and if their heart is touched, they are capable of changing."[12]

The nonviolent action that this love energizes has proven to be one of the most innovative breakthroughs in history. It heals othering, transforms conflict, and unlocks seemingly impossible futures of hope as we'll see in chapter six. Today rigorous political scientists and courageous peace practitioners are convincingly demonstrating its truly world-changing effectiveness.[13]

For Jesus, this groundbreaking work begins in the embodied spiritual practice of calling God our Father.

Beyond Culture and Religion

Jesus illustrates our Father's radical love with one of his most famous stories about a father in conflict with his child. Refreshingly, Jesus was honest about human failure. He didn't suppress or sugarcoat the fact that we often run from God and harm ourselves and others. But Jesus didn't think this ruin needs to be the end of our story or what God wants for us.

The story goes like this.[14]

A son demands his inheritance from his father. In his culture, this request was equivalent to saying, "Dad, I wish you were dead!" Shockingly, the father doesn't disown his son or simply refuse his request. Against all cultural norms, he freely gives his son the inheritance, and the new jet-setter moves far away from home.[15]

The son quickly spends his fortune trying to establish himself in his new community. But after wining and dining with his father's wealth, a famine sets in, and he finds himself outcasted and without food to eat.

Bankrupted and humiliated, the son realizes that he could live a better life as a laborer on his father's farm. So he journeys homeward and anxiously plans to beg his father to accept him back, no longer as a family member but as an indebted servant.

The father's second response is more shocking than the first. He sees his son off in the distance and is *filled with compassion*. He abandons his dignity as an elder in the community and runs to his disgraced son. Despite his filthy clothes that reeked of pigs, the father hugs him and kisses his neck.

The son's apology is soaked in the shame that rattles inside us all. He tells his father, "I am no longer worthy to be called your son." Back home, he offers himself as a devalued tool destined for mere survival.

But his father interrupts his son's shame. He clothes him with his best robe and gives him extravagant gifts. He even gives him a ring, the equivalent of a credit card today. Without saying a word, this father's affectionate embrace embodies the declaration of our divine belovedness: *You are my beloved child; I delight in you.*

In context, this God-embodying father was just as scandalous as his disgraced son. Twice he defiantly disobeyed the biblical imperative to punish his rebellious son with death. In fact, he refused to punish him *at all*. Instead, he exclaims, "Let's have a feast and celebrate!" and throws the boy a party—the very last thing that this bankrupted party animal would seem to deserve. Wrongdoing, resentment, and retribution were washed away with his love. This father saw a lost child in the person condemned by others as a worthless waste and an enemy of moral order.[16]

According to Jesus, *this* father is *our* Father, and *this* embrace is what *divine* love really looks like. God is so filled with compassion that

God rebels against our religious rules. God longs to welcome us home with open arms and lavishes kisses on us even when we bankrupt ourselves. God loves even those most intimate enemies: God's own children who have left God for dead with ingratitude and evil.

Unsurprisingly, then, Jesus scandalized the religious authorities in his society. He publicly declared that our Father's community is wide open to people who have spent their lives cheating others and selling sex. Jesus's practice of partying with outcasts and infidels got him branded as a friend of drunks, traitors, and other "sinners" (Matthew 21:31; 9:11).

In fact, Jesus's belief in God's desire to forgive us was so radical that his dying breath was a cry for God to forgive his own killers. As he hangs on a Roman cross outside Jerusalem, Jesus prays, "Father, forgive them, for they don't know what they're doing" (Luke 23:34).

This is how entirely Jesus's invocation of God as our Father had saturated the depths of his being. The most shatteringly painful moment of his life didn't explode with suppressed hate and hellish condemnation. When Jesus was crushed, he overflowed with a healing river of hope and a new beginning for murderous enemies who seemed worse than worthless.

This river was sourced in Jesus's baptism in divine belovedness. When we pray to Our Father with Jesus, this is the sacred Presence we begin to practice.

Images of a Fierce Tenderness

As we've just seen, Jesus was painfully familiar with human corruption and suffering. Unlike so many religious entrepreneurs, then and now, Jesus never promised that if we say and do the "right" things, our lives will be happy, wealthy, and invulnerable. Jesus stated bluntly, "What people value highly"—money and power—"is detestable in God's sight." He harshly denounced religious hypocrisy and gave sobering warnings about the risks of practicing with him.[17]

But Jesus's honesty about human corruption and our suffering didn't stop him from speaking with even greater confidence about the trustworthiness of God. In fact, it's Jesus's honesty that invests his vision of God's love with enduring credibility for us today. Jesus was speaking from a deeper dimension of divine perception, from that baptized *metanoia* immersed in our Father's words, *You are my beloved child; I delight in you.*

Three of Jesus's images of God beautifully illustrate his vision of God's fierce tenderness.

First, Jesus loved to observe nature, and he spoke more than once about how God cares for the birds—fragile creatures that disappear just as quickly as they arrive. As he watches them fly, Jesus asks, "Are you not much more valuable than birds?" (Matthew 6:26).

The Hebrew scriptures had taught that doing any work on the Sabbath should be penalized with public execution. But Jesus's sacred humanism led him to boldly reimagine this tradition, and Jesus defiantly healed people on the Sabbath. In fact, he declared that humans are "much more valuable" to our Father than any beautiful bird or religious ritual.[18]

Unsurprisingly, Jesus's prioritization of people over religion infuriated his religious leaders. They started demonizing him and looking for an opportunity to assassinate him. But for Jesus, this religion-transcending compassion is the very heart of God. And we receive gentle reminders of it every time we watch the birds.

Second, Jesus spoke even more intimately and taught that our Father numbers the hairs on our heads. This is another one of Jesus's original insights.

Of course, our hairs represent the smallest, most fleeting and fragile aspects of our lives as mortal creatures. They're the parts of ourselves that we lose—often without even noticing and often under the stress of death.[19]

But Jesus teaches that God notices. Our Parent is intimately near us and knows us better than we know ourselves. Nothing is too small for God's concern and care, even our hair. With gentleness and honesty, Jesus confronts our existential fear that we're ultimately abandoned and alone. He comforts us with threefold emphasis and says, "Do not be afraid… Do not be afraid… Even the very hairs of your head are all numbered. So do not be afraid" (Matthew 10:26, 28, 31).

Jesus warned that some of his followers would be "put to death" for practicing with him. Still, he promised that "not a hair of your head will be destroyed." This is an enormously profound distinction in Jesus's vision of human life. All of us will inevitably die, one way or another (Greek *thanatóo*). But with God's love, we will not be destroyed (Greek *apollumi*). Jesus defies the materialistic assumption that death ends us and delightfully insists that somehow even our hair will be saved (Luke 21:17-18).

While I was writing this book, my mother gave me the baby book that she made for my first birthday. As I looked through its pages, I was transported to my past and found a tiny zip-lock bag with locks of my hair in it. She salvaged them from my first haircut. Tears welled up in my eyes.

My mother wanted me to know that I was loved from the beginning—even before I could understand and before she knew who I would become. And so she saved a fleeting part of my past that was seemingly irrelevant to my future. She wanted it to endure as tangible proof of her unconditional love for me. It's one of the most precious gifts I've ever received.

With astonishing tenderness, Jesus says that God does this for each one of us. Perhaps there are baby books with locks of our hair waiting for us when we die and heaven finally embraces us.

Third, Jesus teaches that our Father in heaven assigns angels to watch over "the little ones" and cares intensely for our safety. To others— perhaps even to ourselves—we may seem abandoned, unprotected, and hopeless. But our vulnerability is secretly guarded by unseen presences from God that can be trusted in life and in death. Here Jesus passionately declares, "your Father in heaven is not willing that any of these little ones should perish," a promise we'll return to in chapter seven.[20]

There is fierce tenderness and countercultural joy humming in how Jesus sees and speaks about God. God is the One who values us more than beautiful birds and ancient religious traditions, who numbers our hair, and who assigns angels to guard and guide us home. This is the One that Jesus invites us to call our Father.

The Hands that Hold Us When We Can't Breathe

It was the fierce tenderness of his divine belovedness that sustained Jesus in the worst moment of his life. And it can sustain us in ours, whether it be cancer or conflict or another catastrophe as we'll see again in chapter six.

At the end of his life, Jesus was arrested by an armed militia, tortured by soldiers, and condemned to public execution by the religious and political authorities of his society. Death by crucifixion was designed to physically dismantle and psychologically humiliate victims. It reduced their humanity to a literal breathless pain through asphyxiation.

In those hours of shattering agony, Jesus courageously continued his practice of invoking our Father. As we've seen, Jesus cried out from the cross, "Father, forgive them." And then, with his last breath, Jesus exhaled, "Father, into your hands I commit my spirit" (Luke 23:46).

In this unbearable moment, Jesus was being mocked as a God- forsaken fool who couldn't save himself. But for Jesus, the loving hands of our Father never stop holding us, even when we can't feel them. This divine embrace is stronger than nails hammered through bone into a lynching tree. God's hands can be trusted to hold us even when our world is falling apart and we can't breathe.[21]

And so Jesus lets go of his life with hope, holding on to his own words, "The Father raises the dead and gives them life… no one can snatch them out of my Father's hand." He passes through death as a doorway into a new experience of God and a resurrection of life (John 5:21; 10:29). We witness a person who dies with nothing to prove and nothing to lose.

Jesus's honesty about suffering is both challenging and comforting to me. Calling God our Father doesn't mean that we won't suffer. In fact, it inspires an inclusive, disruptive life of courageous love that many find infuriating and worthy of death. There will be dark nights of our souls in which we feverishly fear that God has forsaken us like the absent father of my friend Ermias. Perhaps at some point, we all get hung up on the cross and scream, "My God, why have you forsaken me?" (Matthew 27:46).

But the practice of calling God our Father with Jesus deepens our resilience and sustains our hope. Our suffering is not the end of our story. The angel is beside us. Our hairs are counted. We will rise again with the birds. Our Father holds us in those world-making hands and will carry us through death into heaven's kingdom where we are safe and finally home.

Our Father Against Patriarchy

Jesus's vision of God as our Father had subversive, countercultural implications as we've seen already. And Jesus didn't hesitate to make these implications explicit and to call for shocking change in his society and ours still today.

Patriarchy is one of the most striking examples. With brilliant irony and mirthful roguery, Jesus deploys the Fatherhood of God to smash the patriarchal order. In prayer, he challenges us to disbelieve in the

Patriarch of a privileged Tribe or the Daddy of an exclusive Club.

Patriarchy literally means the rule (*arché*) of fathers (*pater*)—
pater-arché. It entitles men to rule over others in hierarchical
relationships of command and control. Patriarchal power is often
constructed upon gender roles, race/ethnicity, social status, and
wealth. In Jesus's world and many cultures today, the title "father"
was the linchpin of the patriarchal order and given to religious
teachers, cultural leaders, and national heroes.

But Jesus daringly taught,

> "Don't call anybody on earth 'father,' for you have only one
> Father, the One who is in heaven… Everyone who lifts him-
> self higher than others will be brought low, and whoever
> brings themselves low will be lifted up." (Matthew 23:9-12)

Two-thousand years removed, it's difficult for us to appreciate
the jugular fierceness of Jesus removing the word "father" from
his followers' vocabularies. It would be like telling the university
system to stop using the title "professor" or "doctor" in the medical
world or "president" in politics or "pastor" in churches. "Father"
was *the* authoritative, organizing title in Jesus's patriarchal society—
from the household to the palace to the Temple itself.[22]

And yet Jesus says to *do this*: disavow the word that holds the
patriarchal order together. And disavow it because of who *God* is.
Heaven has something better, and it's intended for everyone on earth.
God is *our* Father, and that means that *we* are *all* God's children—
siblings with *equal* belovedness in God's sacred family. And that
makes hierarchical titles miseducating and defunct. It's worth noting
that *pater* is also the root word of "patriotism," the ism of devotion
to our "fathers" and their land. Jesus tells us to disavow this system.[23]

When heaven comes to earth, our Father lowers the upwardly-mobile
and elevates the down-and-out. In this way, God brings us into face-
to-face relationships on equal footing. The deconstruction of prayer

repositions us from a "master-servant perspective into a person-to-person perspective," as Martin Luther King Jr. so beautifully observed.[24]

Praying with Jesus, then, requires us to disavow and dismantle the taken-for-granted patriarchal system of superior status, exclusive privilege, and oppressive power. What God really wants is "mercy, justice, and integrity" (Matthew 23:23). This is why Jesus reserved his harshest denunciations for entitled authorities who abuse children, outsiders, and the poor at the bottom of the patriarchal pyramid.[25]

Jesus's rejection of patriarchal language and order was one of his most radical teachings as we'll see again in chapter three. It was a moral time-bomb in culture. When we take it seriously, it undermines the foundations of elitism, sexism, racism, and other forms of dehumanization that privilege some as superior and belittle others as inferior. James Baldwin captured the intense implications of Jesus's teaching in *The Fire Next Time*. Baldwin wrote, "If the concept of God has any validity or any use, it can only be to make us larger, freer, and more loving. If God cannot do this, then it is time we got rid of Him."[26]

But Jesus's teaching has rarely been taken seriously throughout Christian history. Patriarchy remains the unsacred operating system in much Christian culture and society around the world today. This ongoing clash between Jesus's ethics and Christian culture highlights the liberating importance of practicing saying *our* Father with Jesus.[27]

When we invoke God as our Father, we unsay the name of any other human *pater*. And so we begin dismantling patriarchal, patriotic, imperial systems that impoverish our shared flourishing.[28]

God's New We

Jesus delightfully deprivatizes God without depersonalizing God. Provocatively, the words "I" and "me" don't occur in Jesus's prayer; it's all plural amidst the singularity of God.

As we learn to unsay patriarchy by calling God *our* Father, Jesus teaches us to speak the language of God's new *we*. This is an expansive, even cosmic "us" in which competitive, polarized identities are surrendered for a larger divine belonging. As the beloved Buddhist monk Thich Nhat Hanh wrote, "We are they."[29]

The radical inclusivity of Jesus's God is on beautiful display when we look at the people that Jesus originally taught to practice calling God *our* Father. Jesus's audience included people who had histories of various diseases and sicknesses. There were people who suffered from severe pain and seizures, people who had experienced mental illness and demonization. They came from Syria, Galilee, the Ten Cities, Jerusalem, Judea, and east Jordan—the Jewish and pagan, the rural margins and urban centers. Jesus's biographer Matthew sums them up as a vast "crowd" (Matthew 4:23-25; 5:1; 7:28).

In other words, Jesus speaks to people from different ethnic groups and nationalities with different skin tones and physical features. They were locals and foreigners. They had different statuses and represented different classes in society. They likely identified with different religious factions and different religions altogether.[30]

Even more concretely, then, these were people who intimately knew suffering and struggle. They were people with traumatic histories of stigma and exclusion. We can be certain that many of these people looked at each other with deep suspicion, entrenched inferiority or superiority, and bitter hatred. Jesus attracted the strangest gathering of enemies.[31]

And it was *these* people that Jesus taught to talk to God as *our* Father. More than likely, this was the first time that many in the crowd that day had said *our* together and so invoked being a *we*. A shared language was forming. In prayer, patriarchal, imperial walls were coming down. Enemies were becoming an unprecedented *us*.

The implications are profound for all of us and our societies still today.[32]

Dr. Paul Farmer, the celebrated global health advocate, said, "The idea that some lives matter less is the root of all that is wrong with the world."[33] When we talk to God with Jesus, we uproot this othering attitude and become part of a new family. We start healing the us-versus-them mindsets and identities that alienate us from others. We realize that no individual or group owns God, and no human being is unrelated or less than another.

Through prayer, then, we start practicing a speech therapy that heals cultural grammars in which some are said to be separated or inferior to ourselves. Ideologies that script imperialism, racism, sexism, and the other isms of death are interrupted by a daily expression of our togetherness in God *our* Father. Praying with Jesus disruptively but delightfully invokes God's new we.

The late Archbishop Desmond Tutu, famous for his uproarious laughter and unwavering protest against oppression, unpacked the implication like this:

> "[T]here are no ordinary people... Each one of us is a very special person, a VSP far more important and far more universal than your normal VIP... All, everyone, everything, belongs. None is an outsider, all are insiders, all belong."[34]

Tutu's rebellious vision of what happens when we call God our Father reminds me of a Buddhist practice known as "the primal vow of great compassion." A medieval Chinese scripture teaches, "Great practice is to say the name of Infinite Light." Saying this divine name was said to unlock "the treasure-ocean of virtues" that energizes "work for the liberation of all beings." The text calls this "other power."[35]

Tutu understood this "other power." When we call God our Father along with Jesus, we unlock a "treasure-ocean of virtues" that energizes us to work for "the liberation of all." New space opens in which "all, everyone, everything, belongs."

This oceanic belovedness is why Karin Sokel could behold even

Osama bin Laden and Adolf Hitler with healing love. It's why my notoriously violent friend Ermias started calling God our Mother and devoted the second half of his life to creating a home for street children. When our eyes are opened, we see that we share the same Parent, our enmity melts, and the walls between us are slowly demolished.

The Quran gives us a similar vision:

> "People, We created you all from a single man and a single woman, and made you into races and tribes *so that you should recognize one another*. In God's eyes, the most honored of you are the ones most mindful of Him."[36] (Quran Sura al-Hujurat 49:11-13, emphasis added)

Women and men share the same Father. So do all races and tribes. And the insiders and outsiders. And the sick and healthy. And the oppressed and powerful. And the spiritually lost and religiously proud. And the poor and rich. And the documented and undocumented. And everyone in between and otherwise.

The practice of talking to our Father with Jesus revolutionizes how we speak, see, and relate to one another with new humanity. We can surrender building our identities on negations and false binaries, no longer defining ourselves by who we're not and what we're against. We realize that we're no longer orphans, aliens, and enemies destined for rivalry. We are we, sacred family—children of our Father who says to all of us, *You are my beloved; I delight in you.*[37]

Once again, the implications are profound and practical. White American Christians who mindfully called God our Father would have passionately rejected the enslavement of their African siblings. German Christians who mindfully called God our Father would have courageously opposed the slaughter of their Jewish siblings. Rwandan Christians who mindfully called God our Father would have rebelliously resisted the massacre of their Tutsi siblings. Their primal vow of great compassion would have unlocked that treasure-ocean of great compassion in which we are reborn as God's new we.

Imagine talking to God today as our Father with the people we are tempted to see as unrelated or less than ourselves. Twenty years of practice have taught me just how revolutionary this truly is. Sometimes when I find myself among strangers—walking down the street, shopping at the grocery store, serving dinner at the homeless shelter—I whisper to myself, *Our Father*. This prayerful practice gives me the other power to remember that I'm not really among strangers but sacred siblings.

Praying to God as our Father unlocks this inclusive, fierce flourishing that can reintegrate us in ways we've hardly begun to imagine and urgently need today.

Begin Here

So who is God according to Jesus?

God isn't an abstract idea, a religious doctrine, or a cultural patriarch. God is our Parent. And before we've said or done anything, God embraces us with words of unconditional affirmation: "You are my beloved children; I delight in you."

Jesus's God loves enemies and wants to welcome us home with celebration rather than punishment. God tenderly values us more than any religious ritual, numbers our hair, and assigns angels to guard over us. God holds us with unseen hands when we suffer injustice and can't breathe. God liberates us from our oppressive systems and invites us into a new we that crosses every boundary, including death itself.

With Jesus, we discover that we are infinitely loved, intimately known, and eternally cared for. God created us, listens to us, and will never let us go. God wants unending relationship with us.

As we talk with Jesus to our Father in heaven, we learn that heaven is the space where all of this is sourced and comes fully alive on earth.

It's not a far-off place somewhere else. It's the enlivening Presence of God in which we are finally at home. And it's meant for all of us, now and always, here on earth, as we'll see in chapter three.

For many of us—perhaps for *all* of us—Jesus's God is more personal and more loving than we often dare to imagine. We are not cosmic accidents or abandoned orphans. Like the once-atheist Dinah Bazer, we discover that we belong, are part of everything, and have the right to be here. Answering the question, "Who is God?" unlocks the only satisfying answer to the question, "Who am I?" I am a beloved child of God. Our souls were created to be bathed in this divine belovedness.

And this means that our most shameful failures, distressing experiences, and devastating losses don't need to define us. They can't finally separate us from God's love and our hope. As we practice praying to our Parent, our gnawing sense of inadequacy and ravaging self-rejection slowly wash away. We can talk back to the sabotaging voices that insist, "You're a piece of sh*t!" and say *Our Father*. Even when we feverishly fear that we're unwanted and abandoned, we're not alone. Our Father's unseen hands still hold us, and we can trust them. Like Jesus, we have nothing to prove and nothing to lose.

Praying with Jesus to our Father, then, is truly a treasure-ocean of virtues. It's a practice of radical dignity, compassion, and hope. It unlocks a healing vulnerability that opens us to accept that we're accepted and to cherish our original goodness. Julian of Norwich wrote, "In this love we have our beginning."[38]

Perhaps like me, you want to stop right here and let this moment be everything. We need to slow down, breathe deeply, and bathe in our divine belovedness. Letting it wash through us is our life's work, and it's worthy of our attention and time. This is where we'll ultimately return at the end of Jesus's prayer.

But stopping here can dangerously drift toward a false familiarity with God. Despite the new we that Jesus invokes, our God-talk easily ends up twisting "God" into a coping mechanism for ourselves and a weapon against others. Where Jesus takes us next is brilliantly surprising and essential to any credible spirituality.

There is more to practice.

Practice Flourishing

1. Find a quiet place and focus on your breathing. Try setting a timer for sixty seconds, five minutes, or a longer amount of time to help you focus your attention.

    a) As you breathe, inhale *Our* and exhale *Father* or *Mother* or *Love*. As you slowly breathe in and out, welcome the presence of God to wash through you and embrace you.

    b) Then shamelessly speak God's message to yourself: "[Your name], you are my beloved child; I delight in you." Allow these words to cleanse and fill your soul. You may feel embarrassed at first, but say and receive these words with pleasure.

    c) Then receive God's call, "[Your name], love your enemies." Don't worry if God's presence remains unfelt or silent. Keep practicing.

2. Practice saying *Our Father* as you walk in your neighborhood, drive on the road, shop at the grocery store, move about your workplace or classroom, flip past the news channel you disagree with, scroll online, or find yourself getting into an argument. Practice reminding yourself that all of these people are your siblings who are made and loved by God just like you. Activate the new we that Jesus invites us into.

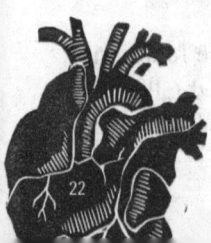

Chapter 2

How Should We Talk About God? Hallowed

A Practice of Radical Reverence

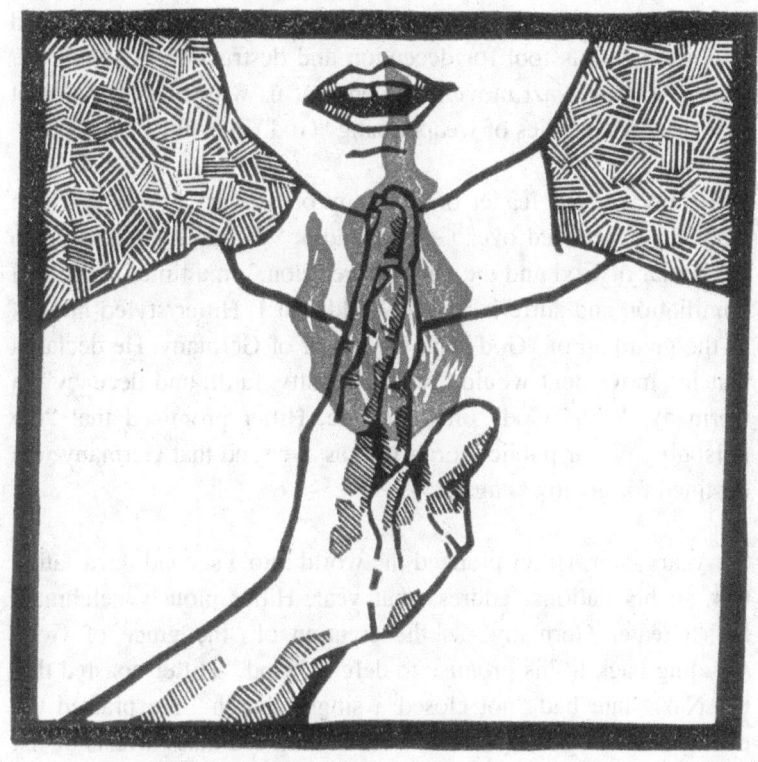

"We have put an end to the denial of God and the abuse of religion."
Adolf Hitler[1]

*"And are we not all that person—we who...cry out
to a god who is but our own ego?"*
Dietrich Bonhoeffer[2]

*"God is nameless... By chattering about God, you tell lies
and commit a sin."*
Meister Eckhart[3]

Weaponizing "God"

Jesus invites us to talk to God as our loving and liberating Parent. Our flourishing begins here in this primal place of our divine belovedness.

But all too easily and often, talk of "God" is badly abused and goes terribly wrong. We're especially vulnerable to this when we feel insecure and under threat. In the worst cases, "God" gets twisted into a dangerous tool for deception and destruction. Adolf Hitler and his fascist Nazi movement confront us with one of the most sobering case studies of weaponizing "God" in history.

Hitler became the leader of Germany on January 30, 1933. Soon after, he announced over German radio, "We have put an end to the denial of God and the abuse of religion." In a time of national humiliation and suffering after World War I, Hitler styled himself as the guardian of "God" and the savior of Germany. He declared that his movement would "restore loyalty, faith, and decency" in Germany. With "God" on their side, Hitler promised that "the poisoning of our public morality" was over and that Germany was destined for greatness again.[4]

Six years later, Hitler plunged the world into a second devastating war. In his national address that year, Hitler piously celebrated his "Greater Germany" as the creation of "the grace of God." Alluding back to his promise to defend "God," Hitler boasted that the Nazi state had "not closed a single church." He praised the events unfolding in Germany—which included mass arrests, racist massacres, and totalitarian terror—as proof of "the Lord Almighty's blessing." Hitler even called himself a "prophet" and promised "the annihilation of the Jewish race in Europe." Alas, invoking "God" and inciting genocide in the same speech is an old trick in the history of political propaganda.[5]

Sadly, Hitler's god-talk was extremely effective. This is what people wanted to hear in their time of vulnerability and desperation. In fact, in some regions of Germany, 89 percent of the *pastors* pledged to be "faithful and obedient" to Hitler in the name of "God."[6] Many of Germany's most rigorous Christian scholars and theologians became enthusiastic Nazis. German society was mobilized by this intoxicating cocktail of "God" and nationalism. From the start, Dietrich Bonhoeffer warned that Hitler's "God" was "nothing but our own ego."[7]

In retrospect, we know the devastating results of what Hitler attributed to "God" and "God's blessing." Totalitarian terror was unleashed. A vicious, scientifically baseless racial ideology was popularized. Six million Jews and other minorities were murdered in unspeakable genocidal horror. And the world was wracked by another catastrophic war.[8]

In the dark shadow of Hitler's death camps—as well as the child abuse in churches today, the corruption of celebrity leaders, and countless other religious scandals—we know all too well that talk of "God" can be dangerous and destructive. Reflecting on our history, the poet Amanda Gorman astutely observes, "Our future needs us / alarmed."[9]

Hallowing God

Jesus presciently understood this need for alarm. He had a sober view of human fallibility and our tendency to invoke "God" for our own corrupt ambitions.

So after inviting us to intimately address God as our Father, Jesus brilliantly interrupts any false familiarity with God. He calls us to wrestle with the disruptive question, "How should we talk about God?"

Jesus's response is fierce and freeing. He teaches us to pray *Hallowed be your name* (Matthew 6:9; Luke 11:2). With these four radioactive words, Jesus sounds an alarm in our ears, sets a refining fire in our mouths, and tests whether our talk about "God" is real or just a ruse for our selves before we say another word. Those who call God our

Father must also name God's otherness, God's transcendence, God's ineffable difference from every human project and power. We must hallow God's name—a practice that Hitler strategically expunged from Jesus's prayer leading up to the Holocaust.[10]

"Hallowed" translates from the Greek verb *hagiazo*. To *hagiazein* something means to recognize its holiness, to acknowledge its right to radical reverence and respect. The hallowed can never be taken for granted or treated presumptuously. As we'll see, it must be approached with utmost attention and awe. Again and again, hallowing leads to silence, the deconstruction of religious hypocrisy, and seemingly impossible liberations from ego and injustice. The Spanish mystic John of the Cross wrote, "Holy things of their own nature cause humility."[11]

In the second movement of his prayer, then, Jesus invites us to re-train our God-talk. Yes, God is our Father. But we must consciously hallow God's name and speak against any attempt to squeeze God into our system, manipulate God as our mascot, or twist God into trump for our tribe. Speaking of God with reverence requires this double-motion of both *delighting* in God's loving Presence and *disavowing* any false grasp on God. With Jesus, we learn by *unlearning* how to say God's name. We rediscover *God* by losing "God."

Jesus's practice of hallowing God's name distills an ancient stream in Hebrew spirituality. This profound tradition reveals the rich depths, challenging intensity, and liberating beauty of Jesus's spirituality. We'll start with a master manipulator named Jacob and work our way forward to Jesus through Hebrew scripture.

Wrestling with the Unnamed Stranger at Peniel

Jacob was a man who wanted to win at any cost. His name literally means Heel-Grasper. This unflattering moniker bluntly captured Jacob's addiction to control and manipulating others. He habitually grasped people at their weakest point, pulled their feet out from under them, and trampled over them for his own advancement.

The outcomes were mixed. Jacob became increasingly wealthy, and his entourage expanded. By all appearances, he was winning. But broken relationships, bitter resentment, and escalating conflict haunt his story. We meet a man seemingly unconscious of consequences. He's both ruthlessly cunning and badly out of control, callously bulldozing over people and cyclically producing pain. Jacob was an addict to his own security.

Not unlike other serial manipulators, Jacob also habitually claimed God's name to justify his selfish schemes. At various points in Jacob's story, "God" seems to function as Jacob's alter-ego, like an invisible puppet that Jacob uses to tell himself what he wants to hear. For Jacob, seemingly everyone—including "God"—was a tool to be used and abused for his own ends.[12]

But Jacob gets stopped in his tracks, and his story takes a surprising turn. In the darkest night of his life, he meets a God that he didn't know and couldn't name. And it's this loss of control that sends him limping toward reconciliation with his worst enemy.

Jacob's mother Rebekah named him Heel-Grasper because he was born gripping the foot of his twin brother Esau. Jacob never accepted being second, and as an adult, he manipulated Esau out of his cultural privilege as a first-born son. Then Jacob shamelessly deceived his father, Isaac. In fact, Jacob pretended to *be* Esau and tricked his blind father into transferring all of Esau's inheritance to himself. Jacob was the original identity thief and scammer.[13]

When Esau discovered this heartless betrayal, he "seethed with resentment." We can feel Esau erupting with burning anger as he curses Jacob's cruel character. That day Esau vowed, "I will kill my brother Jacob" (Genesis 27:30-42).[14]

Jacob had won at last. And he piously credits "God" for his triumph, saying, "God gave me good luck." But Jacob won by wrecking his most intimate relationships. His narcissistic ambition had blinded him to the enraged resentment he was creating. Like an addict, Jacob's success and self-destruction were inseparable (Genesis 27:20).

And so Jacob's only remaining option was to run for his life, and he moves far from home to his uncle Laban's house. But the changed context doesn't change Jacob's character. He embeds himself in the family, begins managing Laban's business, and cunningly siphons off the profits for himself. Soon enough, Laban's sons erupt like Esau and shout with resentment, "Jacob has taken everything!" (Genesis 31:1).

Like an addict doing the same thing and expecting a different result, Jacob does what Jacob knows how to do. He sees himself as an innocent victim, claims "God" is on his side, tells one last lie, and hits the road.[15]

But now Jacob's addiction to winning has driven him into the darkest night of his life. He's left with no option but to travel back toward the brother who had vowed to murder him. And Jacob is rightly terrified that he'll be slaughtered with his entire family. For the first time in his story, we see Jacob acknowledge his own smallness and desperately cry out to God for help.[16]

And God's help comes—but in an unsettling form that Jacob could have never anticipated.

All alone in the darkness of night, a Stranger overtakes Jacob and seizes hold of him. The two men wrestle and struggle against one another. As their breath grows heavy and hearts race, the Stranger asks Jacob for his name. It's here, in his exhausted desperation in the middle of nowhere, that Jacob finally faces himself. He confesses his character as a self-destructive deceiver and manipulator—as the *Heel-Grasper*.

The Stranger then renames Jacob and gives him a new identity: the *God-Wrestler*. He wrenches Jacob's hip, throws him to the ground, and blesses him with this reversal.

Unsurprisingly, Jacob quickly counters by asking for the divine Stranger's name. In the ancient world, a god's name was like a handle that could be used to grasp and control its powers—like a charm or magic spell. In his moment of crisis, Jacob flexes one last time to pin God down as his tool for yet another triumph.

But God refuses to reveal God's name. The God that Genesis calls Elohim resists offering Jacob the illusion of another heel to grasp. Instead, the Stranger turns the questioning around and interrogates Jacob, "Why should you ask my name?" (Genesis 32:29).

For a second time, Jacob is challenged to look inside and confront his addiction to overpowering and using others, including God. At last, this unnamed God slips through his helpless hands and vanishes.

As the sun rises on his day of dread, Jacob is left limping. His prowess is gone, his pride shattered. So Jacob names this holy place Peniel—Hebrew for The Face of God. He memorializes the fact that he couldn't grasp God's power but only caught a glimpse of God's mysterious Presence.[17]

Still, Jacob's dread isn't magically avoided by this divine encounter. Esau appears on the horizon, and four hundred men are with him. A revengeful massacre seems to be in the offing. But the limping God-Wrestler had undergone a conversion, and nothing goes as expected.

Jacob surrenders control at last. He humbly bows to the ground seven times in front of his enraged brother. Esau is so shocked by Jacob's vulnerable act of remorse that Esau runs to him, embraces him, and kisses him. In this powerful moment, the despised Esau becomes the archetype for the merciful father in Jesus's story of divine love. Shattering all expectations, the estranged brothers hold one another and begin to weep.

Jacob's tearful words to Esau are astonishing: "To see your face is like seeing the face of God" (Genesis 33:10).[18] Emmanuel Levinas, the Jewish philosopher and Holocaust survivor, reminds us that every face bears a trace of God. We can glimpse this trace but never control it. Levinas wrote, "The face is a living presence... The face speaks... The face resists possession, resists my powers."[19] The face presents us with Peniel, no longer as a static place but as a sacred person.

Of course, Jacob is looking into the face of his arch-rival whom he had tried to dominate since birth. Esau was the victim of Jacob's heartless betrayal and the enraged enemy who vowed to murder him.

But after wrestling with the unnamed God and bowing to the dust, Jacob sees Esau's face as the divine Face. It now reflects the holy dignity that he had learned that he could never overpower. And so the humbled Heel-Grasper does what seemed impossible just a few hours before: he witnesses and affirms the unnamed God in the face of his enemy.[20]

This is the first time in the Bible that a human being asks for God's name. And it's God's *refusal* to give a name—and God's reversal of asking for *ours*—that proves so life-changing. Narcissistic denial is interrupted by honest confession. The grasping hand is opened to hug the other. Winning gives way to reconciliation. And words of deception and death are converted into shared weeping and divine revelation: *To see your face is like seeing the face of God.*

Against all odds, bitter enemies bury their father in peace as brothers once again. Jacob had finally lost control of "God," and that is how he found our Father.[21]

A Name of Liberation at the Burning Bush

Generations later, one of Jacob's long-great-great-grandchildren asks for God's name again.

Moses was born as a Hebrew slave in the Egyptian empire during a terrifying campaign of genocidal violence. Through courageous acts of Hebrew disobedience and Egyptian empathy, Moses survived the slaughter and was raised in Pharaoh's palace. But after witnessing the oppression of his people, Moses murders an Egyptian slavemaster and, like Jacob, runs for his life.[22]

Decades later, Moses finds himself alone in the wilderness. As he tends his sheep in the shadow of a mountain, he sees a bush burning with flames but unconsumed by the fire. Moses is confounded by this strange sight and steps closer to see if he really sees what he's *seeing*.[23]

A Voice calls out with Moses's name from within the fire:

> "Moses, Moses! Come no closer here. Take off your sandals from your feet, for the place you are standing on is *holy* ground." (Exodus 3:5, emphasis added)

Hallowing centers in our consciousness an appropriate distance: *this is not mine or under my control*. God's holy Presence calls us to stand back with acute attention and radical reverence. It requires a posture of naked vulnerability with bare feet humbly rooted in the dust, like Jacob's face when he bowed before Esau.

This is the first time in the Bible that God is described as a Father. God tells Moses that God has heard the cries of God's enslaved children and "knows their pain." God then gives Moses the daring mission of freeing God's powerless people from the Egyptian empire. Here we find the roots of Jesus's vision of God as a listening Parent with compassion for the abused. Our Father's love disavows oppression and cries out for liberation.[24]

But Moses is unconvinced. He worries that his oppressed people won't believe that he's had a real encounter with God—unless he can tell them God's *name*. So just like Jacob, Moses asks God the ultimate question: "What is your name?" Moses wants a grip on God before he sets off on this impossible mission in a place full of violence and trauma (Exodus 3:13).

But God's answer unsettles Moses like the bush burning right in front of him. God declares, "I-Am-Who-I-Am"—in Hebrew, *Ehyeh-Asher-Ehyeh* or, in shortened form, *Yahweh*. This is a self-asserting Name like the Stranger's face that Jacob glimpsed but couldn't grasp at Peniel. It declares God's liberating Presence but refuses to be possessed by any human power (Exodus 3:14-15).

Professor Michael Fishbane, a renowned Jewish scholar who taught me Hebrew scripture at the University of Chicago, argues that God actually names Godself in the future tense: *I-Shall-Be-Who-I-Shall-Be*. In effect, God is telling Moses that God's name is unspeakable. Only God can speak for Godself as the One who unlocks a new future. God is "the Name beyond names" and always ahead of us, calling us to follow God toward freedom. According to Fishbane, this divine self-revelation was totally unprecedented in the ancient world.[25]

In the looming shadow of Hitler's Holocaust, Dietrich Bonhoeffer summarized the implications of this ungraspable God:

> "The meaning of divine revelation for human religious life is this: There can be no point in human life when we can speak of God as our possession… God is always the One who is to come; that is God's transcendence. One can only have God by expecting God."[26]

But the Hebrews in Egypt had spent four hundred years enslaved to a religion-saturated empire. Like Hitler, Pharoah weaponized Egypt's god-talk to justify and sanction its brutal domination of others. After centuries of suffering, Moses and his people could all-too-easily assume that this new God would follow the old imperial script.

So I-Shall-Be-Who-I-Shall-Be unshackles Godself from this enslaving ideology from the start. The slaves' first act of liberation would be to unlearn the assumption that they could say God's name and weaponize it for themselves, rather than becoming a new we of justice and freedom for others. On hallowed ground, then, Moses hears God declare Godself as the Liberator that no human can comprehend or control. It's as if God names Godself *Exodus*—a

Going-Forth, a Bursting-Out, an I-*Shall*-Be of defiant freedom beyond the grip of any oppressive empire (Exodus 3:15-17).

The Jewish practice of writing God as "G-d" is rooted here. This hallowing practice disruptively reminds humans that all of our sayings of God are hollow. God is never captured by our language or power. The true G-d is always both less and more than we believe—breaking out of our boxes, slipping through our spellings, opening space for the suffering, and crying out for their freedom.

The Black theologian James Cone discerned the spirit of this practice when he wrote, "There is no knowledge of Yahweh except through his political activity on behalf of the weak and helpless."[27] Every other naming of "God" is empty and an ideology that ultimately enslaves.

"My Name Is Unknowable!"

After Israel's liberation from Egypt, the Hebrew scriptures record a third encounter that revolves around the mystery of God's name.

This time, the divine Stranger visits a man named Manoah and his unnamed, infertile wife. To their astonished joy, he reveals that they're going to have a baby and that this miracle child would grow up to lead their people. Manoah is amazed and asks, "What is your name? We should like to honor you when your words come true" (Judges 13:17).[28]

Unlike Jacob and Moses, Monoah's question isn't seemingly motivated by insecurity or incredulity. He says that he wants to *honor* God.

But predictably now, the divine Voice answers with a curt counter-question: "Why do you ask my name?" Manoah's professed desire to honor God is ungloved as Jacob's grasping hand.

In response, God bluntly says, "You must not ask for my name; it is unknowable!"

And with that, "a marvelous thing happened." The Stranger ascended to heaven amidst flames, and the couple—like Jacob before Esau—"flung themselves on their faces to the ground" (Judges 13:18-23).

Jacob isn't given a name at all. Moses gets a name that he can't properly say. And Manoah and his wife hear a defiant declaration of ineffable Mystery: *My name is unknowable!*

"I Am Lost!" or How to Become a Prophet

Moses and Manoah's fiery experiences with God's name anticipate Isaiah's encounter with holy fire.

Isaiah lived in 8th century Jerusalem on the precipice of foreign invasion and a devastating national exile. In this time of crisis, he hears a startling call to become a prophet, someone who speaks on behalf of G-d. Rabbi Abraham Joshua Heschel writes that his new vocation would be "harsh and compassionate, a fusion of contradictions" that "wrenched one's conscience."[29]

Isaiah's society was saturated with religion. By this point, the liberating God of Jacob, Moses, and Manoah had been normalized and nationalized. The people prayed and fasted. They gathered for religious services and offered abundant gifts to God. In return, they made demands of God and expected God to answer them with power and prosperity.

But much like ours today, their religious society was also corrupt and violent. Oppression and indifference to suffering had been normalized right along with "God." Women and children were the greatest victims of this injustice at the bottom of the patriarchal pyramid.[30]

Perhaps unsurprisingly, then, Isaiah needed to be radically undone before he could speak as a prophet of *G-d* and not just another religious profiteer. His pious theology needed to be purged. And that's exactly what Isaiah experiences in his call to become a prophet.[31]

Israel's king had recently died, and the nation teetered on the edge of invasion. Amidst this loss and surging insecurity, Isaiah has an experience of God like never before. He hears the booming voices of heavenly beings hallowing God's name with cries of "Holy! Holy! Holy!" He feels the ground quake beneath his feet, and he's engulfed in smoke (Isaiah 6:3).

With his taken-for-granted orientation totally upended, Isaiah expresses what is exploding within him. He erupts with the cry, "Woe to me! I am lost!" (Isaiah 6:5a).

The holy Presence of God had utterly deconstructed him. The thunderous hallowing of God's name had made him acutely aware of the hollowness of his and his society's God-talk. Isaiah desperately confesses, "I am a man of unclean lips, and I live among a people of unclean lips"—mouths that meaninglessly manipulated God's name for human power (Isaiah 6:5b).

A heavenly creature then touches Isaiah's lips with a fiery coal and symbolically burns away his mouth's corruption. Nothing less severe could suffice for his prophetic vocation.

This hallowing experience radically remade how Isaiah spoke about God. His passionate prophecies reverberate with it as he calls God *the Holy One* no less than thirty times in the book that bears his name. With tenderness and tenacity, Isaiah insists on God's transcendence and declares, "As the heavens are high above the earth, so are My ways high above your ways and My plans above your plans" (Isaiah 55:9).

And God's plans become a holy roar of prophetic protest in Isaiah's mouth. The ruined-yet-refined prophet goes on to boldly denounce his society's religious gatherings, offerings, and prayers as meaningless to G-d. He lifts up compassion for the lowly and equitable justice for all as the very heart of God. And in a time of national siege, Isaiah does the unthinkable and traitorously announces the inclusion of Israel's enemies as God's ultimate dream for God's war-torn family.[32]

Isaiah embodied what Rabbi Heschel wrote about all true prophets:

> "Instead of showing us a way through the elegant mansions
> of the mind, the prophets take us to the slums... To us a
> single act of injustice—cheating in business, exploitation
> of the poor—is slight... [But] to the prophets it is a death-
> blow to existence... a threat to the world."

And so Isaiah courageously speaks with "the voice that God has
lent to the silent agony."[33] His message booms with the liberation
echoing back to Jacob's encounter with the unnamed God and his
enemy at Peniel. Isaiah distills this stream into its most potent
expression in history:

> "Raise your voice like an alarm! Shout it out loud! Jacob's
> children have rebelled! They pray every day and seem eager
> to know me.

> But they exploit their workers. They argue and attack one
> another.

> Unlock the chains of injustice and set the oppressed free!
> Share your food with the hungry, clothe the naked, and
> shelter the poor in your homes!

> Then you will pray, and I-Shall-Be will answer." (Isaiah
> 58:1-12, my paraphrase)

Hebrew Hallowing

These four stories in Hebrew scripture unfold across different contexts
and distant centuries. But they sketch a strikingly similar pattern.

First, humans habitually want to know God's name. We're addicted to labeling God and grasping for a handle to capture and control God's power.

Second, we present seemingly good and even pious reasons for why we need this religious vice grip. Jacob feared for his life. Moses was called to emancipate an enslaved people. Manoah wanted to give thanks for a miracle.

But, third, God always resists giving God's name. With Jacob, God questions why he wants to know, renames *him*, and sends him limping toward reconciliation with his enemy. With Moses, God gives an unspeakable name that outruns him toward liberation for suffering people. With Manoah and his wife, the Voice questions their question and protests, "My name is unknowable!"

By the time we get to Isaiah, the undone prophet doesn't even ask for God's name. Hearing the hallowing of God compels him to confess his corrupted speech and kiss the burning coal. He then courageously critiques his culture's self-serving religion and calls for a return to the liberating God of Jacob who transforms enemies into family.

With each turn of this pattern, we learn that God's name is holy. To hallow God requires radical reverence and the conscious sobriety that God cannot be pinned down by human power for human ambition. God defies our religious lust for labels and convenient certainty. God demands that we follow G-d in humility toward reconciliation and justice with those we have betrayed, belittled, and oppressed. A changed way of life marked by compassion and justice is the only credible proof that we've met with our Father and can speak on God's behalf—not a religious language game.

Any other naming of "God" lies and enslaves. Hitler's arrogant claim to defend God while weaponizing "God" against the Jewish people is just one devastating example of many throughout history. The Hebrew tradition repeatedly alarms us and warns that this "God" must be disavowed for the dangerous delusion that it is.

Here we find ourselves in the heart of the Bible's Ten Commandments. The first declares our Father's living, liberating Presence and denounces imperial gods. The second forbids humans from fabricating idols to fake God as a religious tool. The third addresses how we talk about God: "You shall not take the name of the Lord your God in vain." Reverent refusal to misuse God's name is the dialect of any credible sacred community. Everything else is meaningless and dangerous (Exodus 20:7; Deuteronomy 5:11).

A book late in Hebrew scripture summarizes the radical reverence that talking about God requires. The author of the book, only ever called "the Teacher," says,

> "Go near to God to listen rather than to offer the sacrifices of fools, who don't know that they do wrong. Don't be quick with your mouth; do not be hasty in your heart to utter anything before God. God is in heaven and you are on earth, so let your words be few... Reverence God." (Ecclesiastes 5:1-2, 7)

Jesus Deconstructs Hollow God-Talk

"Hallowed be your name," Jesus teaches us to pray. As a brilliant teacher of Hebrew scripture, Jesus distills this ancient stream of (un)speaking of God into these four radioactive words.

This hallowing of God's name reverberated in Jesus's own rugged deconstruction of hollow religious language. In the same teaching in which Jesus introduced his prayer, Jesus warned,

> "Not everyone who says 'Lord! Lord!' to me will get into the kingdom of heaven. Only the one who does the will of my Father who is in heaven can enter. On that day, a lot of people will say to me, 'Lord! Lord! Didn't we prophesy in your name, and didn't we drive out demons in your name, and didn't we do many miracles in your name?' Then I'll

tell them straight up, 'I never knew you. Get away from me, you evildoers!'" (Matthew 7:21-23; see John 17:11-12)

Of course, "Lord" was the pious name for Yahweh in Jesus's culture. And prophesying, driving out demons, and performing miracles were considered the premium proof of an exceptional connection with God. People who talked and performed like this would seem like the ultimate insiders with God who can be trusted to speak for God.

But Jesus, like Isaiah before him, defiantly disagrees. Instead, he insists that piously saying God's name—even saying it to Jesus himself!—and performing amazing miracles are meaningless, if they're disconnected from "the will of my Father in heaven."

This statement signals something profound and provocative in many religious circles: our Father's ultimate *will* is something more basic and difficult than simply preaching God's name and performing spectacles. As Jacob experienced, Isaiah promised, and Jesus made explicit, our Father's will is for us to love our enemies as sacred siblings in God's family. This prophetic *we* reveals the very heart of God and the entire vision of the Bible.[34]

Without this, scripture unravels, and Jesus unmasks what we face with Hitler. We can charismatically claim God's name—even promise to *guard* God's name and secure church culture. In the process, we may succeed in rallying millions of religious people to our cause. And yet in doing so, we may unleash terrible evils that desecrate G-d's name and destroy G-d's beloved family. Pinning "God" to our cause is zero proof that it actually reflects who *G-d* is or what *G-d* really wants.

Thankfully, Jesus pinpoints three telltale signs that help us sound out empty god-talk: (1) being certain that we're right, (2) looking down on others, and (3) expressing pride in our religious identity. Conversely, spiritual authenticity is indicated by radical reverence. This humility (1) avoids the spotlight, (2) looks down on no one, and (3) confesses our fallibility and need for divine mercy (Luke 18:9-14).

Jesus's wisdom of hallowing is counter-intuitive but essential for our flourishing. It alarms us to the fact that those who talk about God with the most certainty may be worthy of our greatest suspicion. And it reminds us that the ones we hold in greatest suspicion but who humbly ask for God's help may be right before God.

Hallow G-d

The first two movements of Jesus's prayer lead us into the practice of a paradox, a stretching spiritual tension that strengthens our flourishing.

From one side of our mouth, we can confidently and affectionately talk to God as our Father. This is who God is, loving and liberating. God embraces us with delight and calls us beloved.

But from the other, we must hallow G-d's holy name and never talk about G-d with hubris. In fact, we must actively deconstruct human claims to comprehend or control "God" for our causes.

Practiced together, these two movements of prayer cultivate a credible, critical spirituality. God is personal but never private, present but never possessed. God declares us beloved but dismantles our boxes. God infinitely values us but vanishes whenever we devalue others. We can say *our* Father but must hallow *Your* name.

An older man recently admitted to me, "I don't like tension." I appreciated his refreshing honesty; tension is unsettling to me too. But we cannot truly flourish without this spiritual tension that Jesus invites us to straddle.

Contemporary spirituality addictively slouches toward an indulgent and gullible "God" that is little more than our own ego. Jacob is grasping after all of us, and we rightly struggle against him. But our reaction to religious abuse easily silences God altogether. We find ourselves sinking into a secularism that shrinks the horizon of our humanity toward hopelessness.

Jesus's spiritual practice pioneers a better path for us today. He trains us to inhabit God's intimate tenderness and God's interrupting otherness. This tension leads us into the saving-yet-unsettling Presence of God at Peniel. The unnamed Stranger wrestles us out of our self-serving religion and sends us limping toward our enemies with healing words: *Seeing your face is like seeing the face of God*.

When we can say *this*, fierce flourishing ignites in our mouths, and we can speak of God with justice. Every person becomes Peniel, and the new we that Jesus invokes finds its voice.

The stakes are high. Hitler exchanged hallowing for hatred, and an historically Christian society hardly noticed. Millions were mobilized for mass violence in the name of their genocidal "God" and the empty promise of national "greatness." Horrific evil was unleashed that haunts us to this day. Are we better than they?

We need to be alarmed by the rumble of radical reverence. We need to lose "God" to find G-d again. We need the hallowing mind of Bonhoeffer, the Nazi-resister who confessed, "to have God means to realize that human beings can never have God."[35]

Still, stopping here can strand us in deconstruction. The unlearning that it unlocks is a crucial step in our journey. But it's not the destination. We need to keep moving with Jesus, lest we get stuck in a purely critical and passive spirituality.

There is more to practice.

Practice Flourishing

1. When you say or hear "God," "Lord," "Father," or other names for holy Mystery, train your mind to add, *Hallowed be your name*. Then cross-examine how God's name is being used and whether it reverences God's otherness or reveals human opinion and ambition.

2. Start writing "G-d" in texts, emails, and posts. If you're asked why you do this, explain that it's a simple practice that helps you stay alert and remember that God's name always means more and less than we assume.

Chapter 3

What Do You Want?
Your Kingdom Come

A Practice of Prophetic Imagination

> *"Whoever rules, our duty to the City*
> *is loyal opposition, never greening*
> *for the big money, never neighing after*
> *a public image…*
> *[T]o serve as a paradigm*
> *now of what a plausible Future might be*
> *is what we're here for."*
> **W.H. Auden**[1]

Imagination: Humanity's Greatest Superpower

Once we bathe in our divine belovedness and G-d breaks out of our religious boxes, where Jesus takes us next in prayer is as wide as the world.

Imagination is probably humanity's greatest superpower. Yes, we stand erect with consciousness, language, reason, and technology. But all of this comes together in our imagination. Psychiatrist Bessel van der Kolk writes, "Imagination is absolutely critical to the quality of our lives."[2] It's why we have new futures rather than endless replays of the past.

Imagination is how our engineering has developed from cobbling mud huts in rural villages to constructing skyscrapers in global cities. It's how medicine has shifted from amputating legs and locking people away in asylums to installing prosthetic limbs and pioneering mental health. It's how our politics has progressed from conquering empires to multicultural democracies—if they have. It's how we've got eyeglasses, antibiotics, pizza, Harry Potter, *To Pimp a Butterfly*, the Internet, smart phones, space travel, and nuclear energy.[3]

And desire is the rocket fuel of human imagination. Our discontents dislodge what's familiar, and our desire drives us forward toward what's possible. We start imagining something new and take risks of starting over, casting ourselves into the anxiety of uncertainty and the passion of hope.

If imagination is the horizon of our desire, desire is our spaceship into new worlds.

Of course, the outcomes are inherently unpredictable. Desire and imagination are how we've got global warming but also life-saving treatments for cancer. They're how we've unleashed hideous holocausts but also how we've abolished slavery and established human rights, in many of our law codes at least.

This unpredictability signals the radioactive stakes of what we desire and how we dream. The consequences can be extraordinary— and apocalyptic.

Imagination and desire, then, are where Jesus takes us next. His third movement of prayer invites us into his dream, into the ultimate imagination and desire of God. Jesus names this *the kingdom of heaven*.

Kingdom is an old word for the nexus of imagination and desire. Simply put, it's the combination of what we imagine, what we want, and what we're willing to fight for. As we'll see, the kingdom Jesus imagines is surprising and often subversive to our own, offering a universal belonging and ultimate hope.

So *What do you want?* is the question burning in Jesus's third spiritual practice. It's a question that Jesus often asked people and that Jesus asks us still today. What do we imagine for our lives and planet? What desire is driving us forward? What endgame do we hope is finally accomplished when everything is said and done?

With prophetic passion, Jesus ignites our desire, expands our imagination, and invites us to pray with him, *Let Your kingdom come on earth as it is in heaven* (Matthew 6:10; Luke 11:2). What Jesus meant and how we can be part of it is what this chapter is all about.

Start Over with *Metanoia*

Soon after his baptism, Jesus launched his public movement with the declaration, "Change your mind! The kingdom of heaven is so close!" (Matthew 3:2, 7; 4:17). In fact, Jesus was borrowing the message of his radical cousin John, who baptized Jesus when heaven opened and God said, "You're my beloved son; I delight in you."

John was a courageous reformer, and he was quickly jailed and beheaded for his fearless critiques of Herod's corrupt power. But

Jesus defiantly took up John's message anyway, and he started mainstreaming it everywhere he went.

That word which often gets translated as "repent" is the crucial on-ramp to the kingdom. What *metanoia* really means is a revolution in the mind. It's a call to reset how we imagine and what we desire. *Metanoia* signals the paradigm shift that's required to dream with G-d.

Of course, today we're allergic to the word "kingdom," and rightly so. It conjures up musty memories of royal privilege for a few, inferior status for the many, and violent domination for everyone else who refuses to submit to this hierarchical order. We're all too familiar with patriarchal systems and oppressive empires. Remember chapters one and two? Thankfully, by using the word, Jesus isn't asking us to buy into an obsolete past but to open ourselves to a new future.

This is why Jesus's moral imagination has been called "the upside-down kingdom" and why Jesus always announced it with his call to *metanoia*.[4] He said that entering the kingdom of heaven is like being reborn and becoming a beginner again—like learning how to walk and talk for the first time. It's ultimately something that comes to us and that sets us free to belong together—the polar opposite of something we can control and impose on others.[5]

This is also why Jesus said that the kingdom of heaven is so infinitely precious. It unlocks that treasure-ocean of virtues that energizes radical love and defiant hope. Jesus himself described it as a "treasure" of "fine pearls" that's hidden in an abandoned slum but that's worth selling everything to buy. The kingdom of heaven is the minority vision that justly fills our imagination and fuels our flourishing, now and always.[6]

But it comes at a high price and disrupts the status quo, especially for those bought-in to human empire. Jesus celebrated that the kingdom is wide open to outcasts, sexual deviants, and cultural traitors. Despised and displaced as they were, these people were humble and hungry for a different order of things. *Metanoia* echoed in their ears like a blessing rather than a burden.[7]

In fact, as we've seen, the last act of Jesus's revolutionary life was promising the kingdom to a desperate political rebel as the religious and political authorities executed them outside Jerusalem. When the dying man pleaded with Jesus, "Remember me when you enter into your kingdom," Jesus answered, "Today you will be with me in paradise" (Luke 23:42). Here we catch a glimpse of the kingdom's truly radical rebellion: amidst an excruciating death, Jesus promises a new future to a deadman condemned to annihilation.

No wonder, then, why so many people felt threatened by Jesus's movement. Jesus warned that the old guard and entitled insiders — whether by ethnicity, culture, religion, or some other status — may find themselves unable to accept G-d's kingdom. Its critical imagination and countercultural desire represent an upheaval to privilege and power. Predictably, the kingdom that Jesus announced and embodied was quickly demonized, criminalized, and condemned. As James Baldwin wrote, "Precisely at the point when you begin to develop a conscience, you must find yourself at war with your society."[8]

So *metanoia* is the sacred passage to heaven's kingdom. Without it, we'll overlook the kingdom just like we do our slums today. Or we'll colonize and weaponize it to expand our empires, as has happened so often since Jesus was lynched for it.

Jesus talked about the kingdom fifty times, making it the central theme of his teaching. In the sections below, I'll summarize his beautiful vision with five signs to orient our imagination and energize our desire for practice today.[9] This deep dive into Jesus's moral imagination will land more concretely in chapters six and seven.[10]

Sign 1: Countercultural Love

To understand God's kingdom, we need to work backwards. The last sign is really the first and shows us the heart of all the others. It takes us back to Jesus's baptism and re-immerses us in our divine belovedness, especially when we're afraid that we're failed and finished.

Jesus said surprisingly little about the end of the world. But the single story he tells about it reveals the soul of God's kingdom. And that soul is countercultural love. As Howard Thurman wrote, "The religion of Jesus makes the love-ethic central."[11]

Here's the story.[12]

On the last day of history, "all the nations" of the world are gathered before the King's throne for final judgment. This is the global moment when God's ultimate desire and what lasts forever is unveiled for literally everyone to see.

The King declares to those on his right, "Come, you who are blessed by my Father. Take your inheritance: the kingdom prepared for you since the creation of the world." The King then explains why these particular people belong:

> "I was hungry and you gave me something to eat. I was thirsty and you gave me something to drink. I was a foreigner and you invited me in. I needed clothes and you clothed me. I was sick and you looked after me. I was in prison and you came to visit me." (Matthew 25:35-36)

The citizens of the kingdom then confess their confusion. They don't remember ever seeing or serving the King in these desperate conditions. And, refreshingly, they're honest enough to admit it.

Their confusion leads to the climax of the story. The King answers, "Whatever you did for one of the least of these siblings of mine, you did for me" (Matthew 25:40).

Shockingly, the King in the privileged position of ultimate Judge identifies himself with abused and abandoned people: *they* count for *him*. And so the kingdom's citizens actually embraced the King whenever they embraced *these* people, even though they didn't realize it.

For Jesus, love is what matters and saves, not spiritual transactions to get an inside connection with "God." As the African theologian Augustine wrote, "If God is love, whoever loves love loves God."[13]

The kingdom's revaluation of the unwanted and those who love them shouldn't surprise us. Recall that Jesus began by teaching us to talk to God as *our* Father. And so he calls the erased and excluded nobodies precious *sisters* and *brothers* in God's kingdom. They're at the heart of God's new *we*.

So this is how the citizens of the kingdom get identified when all the masks finally come off: they practice divine belovedness with people who are hungry, thirsty, foreign, unclothed, sick, and incarcerated. They cherish and embrace unwanted people as embodiments of God. They see Peniel—the Face of God—in *these* people, even if they wouldn't say it that way.

Like traditional Christianity teaches, then, Jesus indicates that our belonging in the kingdom is based on how we respond to divinity. But Jesus slants this orthodoxy in a surprising way. True divinity isn't primarily accessed in pious prayers and religious services addressed to the unhallowed "God" that Isaiah critiqued. True divinity is found in suffering people and the love that beholds them as precious. The disinherited are the gatekeepers of the kingdom.

I've lived much of my adult life working in a war-torn country surrounded by failed states in a region that mass-produces refugees and traffics in human bodies. The people Jesus names in this story sound to me like victims of war. They've lost everything and are utterly dependent for their most basic needs. They're stripped of any status or recognizable belonging. They're what we today call stateless persons without any documentation. They've contracted diseases and been punished by the state.

We've seen already that Jesus grew up in an occupied territory of Rome's violent empire. He himself was one of these people—from his earliest memories as a displaced massacre survivor until his state-sanctioned execution. So Jesus boldly names these suffering people as the first citizens of God's kingdom. They're also the key to enter it for everyone else.[14]

I also spend regular time with people at a homeless shelter called Hesed House. Many of these people have histories of devastating loss, severe trauma, mental illness, drug addiction, and prison time. As Derek slowly smoked a cigarette in the cold, he told me about the death of his seven-year-old daughter Jessica. He was estranged from his wife, she was addicted to drugs, and Jessica wasted away until she died. Derek's eyes filled with tears, and his drunken voice slurred as he told me, "I've hit rock bottom."

The kingdom's VIP list reminds me of Jessica, Derek, and the people at Hesed House. Jesus's practice of hanging out with people like them is how he got his infamous reputation as a "friend of drunks and sinners." As we've seen, the audience who originally heard Jesus teach his prayer included survivors of trauma and mental illness. In fact, Jesus experienced homelessness himself and attracted homeless people like a magnet.

In each of them, Jesus saw Peniels and the inheritors of God's dream for the world. And so he says that the kingdom welcomes people so overwhelmed with loss, so mentally ill, so felonized and afflicted that they can't even keep clothes on their backs or a roof over their heads. The kingdom of heaven is the place where *these* people are family and finally feel at home.[15]

For everyone else, embodying love for these sacred sisters and brothers is the key to the kingdom. If these are the kinds of people you champion and dream of being lifted up, you'll be overjoyed and at home in the kingdom too. If you don't really care or think they don't deserve it, God's kingdom may not be the place you want to be forever. Here we see again the centrality of our desire and the fierceness of Jesus's honesty: some of us don't actually *want* this to happen (Matthew 25:41-46).

But Jesus insists that it will, and he beautifully promises that the kingdom will gather Peniels—glimmers of God's Face—from the four corners of the earth. In the end, the kingdom will be the ultimate global party where strangers are reunited as a family of countercultural love and the earth's full diversity. This is where it all ends. This is God's dream.[16] Martin Luther King called it "cosmic companionship."[17]

In his subversive stories about the kingdom, then, Jesus revolutionized how people saw themselves and one another. God's new we was truly being born. Together they discovered a shared dignity and divine destiny defiantly beyond the domination of the human kingdoms that demoralized and discarded them. They too were beloved, sharing a promise of flourishing when God's will wins out. This is why Jesus called the kingdom "good news" in an age of cold-hearted love. The expendable ones end up winning the jackpot.[18]

So countercultural love is where the kingdom begins and ends. It's the soul of the universe in which the nobodies belong and the blacklisted are blessed. It's happy news for the hopeless and an invitation to a global party that never ends.

What do you want? Jesus ignites our desire and invites us to passionately pray, *Your kingdom come on earth as it is in heaven.*

Sign 2: Mutual Relationship

If countercultural love is the soul of God's kingdom, then mutual relationships are its bone structure. The kingdom challenges human hierarchies and overcomes patriarchal power. It replaces them with shared dignity and responsibility on an equal playing field.

This sign of the kingdom takes center stage in a conversation between Jesus and the mother of two of his closest students. I'll call her Salome. Salome approaches Jesus with a request, and he asks her that ultimate question of human desire: *What do you want?* (Matthew 20:21).

Salome responds by asking Jesus to give her sons special positions in the kingdom of God—essentially to make them his vice presidents. She's earnest and expectant. We see her kneeling imploringly in front of Jesus.

Salome's request makes perfect sense within the operating system of our world: get an inside connection, work your way to the top, and secure privilege and power for your tribe. Then and now, many people assume this is what's worth asking for if you can get what you really want.

Jesus's response is striking. He explains that he understands this is how human kingdoms operate. The "rulers" "lord over" others and leverage their "authority." They build hierarchical relationships governed by status and submission defined by superiority and inferiority. Kingdoms with this structure fuel privilege for insiders, resentment for outsiders, and conflict between them (Matthew 20:25; Mark 10:38).

But Jesus explains to Salome that the kingdom of heaven has a totally different structure and subverts this human hierarchy. In the kingdom, real leaders are the ones who are most available, most vulnerable, and most willing to serve those at the bottom. With deviant joy, Jesus says that they operate like unentitled youth who happily include and empower others. This is their "greatness" and Jesus's personal paradigm: "Sacrifice everything over personal gain," as Kendrick Lamar paraphrases. They ensure that others have a place at the table—not that their thrones are secure.[19]

The mutuality of the kingdom takes us back to Jesus's warning not to call anyone "father" except *our* Father. As we saw in chapter 1, the title "father" or *pater* was the lynchpin of the patriarchal system of privilege, resentment, and conflict. Earning that title and exploiting its benefits was—and often still is—the typical goal of a successful man's life. It's what most men imagined and wanted for themselves. Of course, this wasn't even an option for women, though Salome thought she could reap the rewards through her sons.

But if God is *our* Father and if God prioritizes the people that Jesus said God does, then God's kingdom can't be organized in this top-down, command-and-control structure. Jesus levels our relationships and says,

> "You're all siblings... Everyone who lifts himself higher than other folks will be brought low, and whoever brings themselves low will be lifted up." (Matthew 23:8-12)

The kingdom raises the lowly, lowers the high-and-mighty, and the result is equity. It's face-to-face relationship on a level playing field.

This leveling of cultural hierarchy gets repeated in Jesus's statement that children—not fathers—are the secret owners of the kingdom. These "little ones" have yet to be miseducated by who's in and who's out, who's above and who's below. Jesus bluntly warns the rest of us, "Anyone who won't receive the kingdom of God like a little kid will never enter it." Our egos need to become smaller and younger to share space with others in the kingdom (Mark 10:14-15).

Jesus's vision of God's kingdom, then, was a wondrous wrecking ball in his status-driven culture and ours today. Jesus says the kingdom is like workers picking up their paychecks and being shocked to find out that everyone gets paid the same amount. The senior workers resentfully protest, "You have made them equal to us!" But the boss (God) answers, "Don't I have the right to do what I want with my own money? Or are you envious because I'm generous?" (Matthew 20:10-16).

Jesus bluntly names here what many of us feel. The kingdom's mutual equality can make people feel uncomfortable, cheated, and even outraged. We feel entitled to our privilege. But a generous mutuality is what our Father wants, and this is a primary sign of the kingdom's presence on earth.

A clash of kingdoms is coming into view here:

> Human kingdoms tag people with titles that create distance between us based on gender, age, wealth, status, and much besides. God's kingdom disavows these titles.

> Human kingdoms organize themselves with hierarchical relationships of superior and inferior. God's kingdom upends these structures and makes us equals who stand face-to-face.

> Human kingdoms produce nepotistic privilege and envious conflict. God's kingdom prizes sacrifice and equity.

> Human kingdoms immortalize the winners who take all. God's kingdom immortalizes the losers and those who share what they have.

So restructured relationships of mutuality are what Jesus is inviting us to imagine when we pray, "Your kingdom come on earth as it is in heaven." For Jesus, this is the only truly satisfying answer to the ultimate question, *What do you want?*

Sign 3: Integrated Healing

If the soul is love and the body is mutuality, the work of the kingdom is integrated healing: healed bodies, healed minds, and healed relationships. Jesus not only taught the kingdom; he touched people with it, and the outcome was always a new wholeness and human re-membering.[20]

After Jesus's cousin John was jailed for his message of *metanoia*, John sends his students to ask Jesus, "Are you really the one who is to come"—the King who would bring the kingdom? Apparently, even John was starting to be confused by Jesus's surprising stories and lifestyle. He wanted to know if Jesus was really launching God's dream for the world or not (Matthew 11:2).

Jesus responds by showing rather than telling. He invites John's students to look at the outcomes of his movement and judge for themselves. He answers:

> "Blind people get their ability to see. Crippled people walk. People with leprosy get a clean bill of health. Deaf people can hear. Dead people are raised from the dead. And good news gets announced to the poor. Whoever doesn't stumble over me and fall is fortunate." (Matthew 11:5-6)

For Jesus, this is what the kingdom's presence looks like: healing for broken bodies, healing for the stigmatized and excluded, healing for people trapped in powerlessness and death. When these things are happening, the kingdom is already present.

Here we see that Jesus's healings are not just miracles for individuals that delightfully defy a closed, mechanistic worldview. That's a recent and very modern way of understanding what's so miraculous about these miracles. The point for Jesus is the radical social reintegration that heals relationships and communities. This is why Jesus focuses on these healings when John asks if he's bringing the kingdom. He wants John to reimagine what the kingdom actually looks like.

For example, Jesus often spent time with people who had mental illness and helped them heal. When he did this, Jesus certainly healed people's relationships with their own selves. They were no longer compulsively possessed and splintered but reconciled within themselves.

But in doing this, Jesus also healed people's relationships *with others*. They were no longer othered and excluded. In their healing,

Jesus could say to them, "Return home and describe how much God has done for you." These were precious words for outcasts that previously seemed impossible to hear. *Return home* and tell the story of how your life has divine value (Luke 8:39).

In my neighborhood in Addis Ababa, I frequently see people with mental illness who walk the streets completely naked. Their hair is matted, their skin is calloused, and their bodies are exposed. Some people pity them. But others stare and laugh at them. Most people fear and avoid them. The thought of these "crazy" people returning home is almost unimaginable.

But this is exactly what Jesus offered to people who were naked and homeless, splintered and stigmatized. He shared a healing that reconciled them to themselves *and* that gave them the gift of returning home to others.

We see again that God's dream looks like a reintegrated *we*, both within and between our selves. When we look carefully, all of Jesus's healings have this holistic, reconciling dimension. They simultaneously restore personal dignity, agency, and community. They open the way to our deepest desire: *home*.

Jesus called this integrated healing the clearest sign that heaven is coming to earth. The kingdom not only reintegrates individuals with themselves and people with their communities. It also reintegrates heaven and earth, the way the world is meant to be with the way it really is. The kingdom remarries our highest hopes and life as we know it.[21]

So praying "Your kingdom come *on earth as it is in heaven*" is audaciously praying for the reintegration of reality, for a cosmic healing that isn't just for a far-off place in another time but something that begins *here and now*. When heaven opens, Jesus hears healing words of divine belovedness wash over him. When heaven is welcomed, earth comes alive. Mental health returns. Bodies are restored. Home reopens for the rejected.

If you're sick of the brokenness and ache for healing, Jesus says that the kingdom is for you. We can taste it now and trust in its full arrival in the end. He invites us to soak our imagination in it, to desire it, and to partner in its coming.

But if you benefit from the brokenness, Jesus warns that the kingdom will feel intensely threatening.

Sign 4: Nonviolent Witness

This backlash is exactly what Jesus experienced, and it's why he warned John's students against "stumbling" over him like a rock in the road. When you share healing with people, those who benefit from their brokenness won't be happy. The kingdom doesn't come via the nationalistic identity, military power, and socio-economic privilege that many associated with it.[22]

And so Jesus's kingdom was seen as dangerous. Soon enough, the cultural guardians arrest Jesus and accuse him of "subverting our nation." Jesus rechanneled people's loyalty to another desire, and this made him *persona non grata*, a public enemy. One of the top religious leaders cynically stated that Jesus had to be stopped to "save the nation" (Luke 23:2; John 11:50).

Here we face one of the most challenging signs of God's kingdom, which I'll explore further in chapter six: *nonviolent witness*. This is where our trust in the kingdom is severely tested.

After three short years of public work, Jesus was arrested and beaten by a militia. He was then handed over to Pilate, the Roman governor of Jerusalem, who proceeded to interrogate him. Pilate's lead question pinpointed the traitorous charge against Jesus: "Are you the king of the Jews?" If Jesus claimed kingship, then he had denied Caesar's sovereignty and condemned himself to death (John 18:33).

More than likely, Pilate expected Jesus to crumble, confess his disloyalty, and grovel for mercy. If Jesus did this, he would incriminate himself, humiliate the Jewish people, and reaffirm Pilate's power.

But Jesus answered defiantly:

> "My kingdom isn't based on this world's system. If it were, my people would fight to prevent my arrest by the Jewish leaders. But now my kingdom is from another place." (John 18:36)

Notice three things in Jesus's rebellious response.

First, Jesus claims that he actually has a kingdom. He defies Pilate, Caesar, and the religious leaders who arrested him.

But, second, Jesus states that his kingdom is not governed by the world's system of violence and domination. It has a different origin and operating system far beyond human power. It comes "from another place" that the empire couldn't colonize.

So, third, Jesus refuses to use violence to secure his kingdom. He resists playing Pilate's game and doesn't need his allies to fight to save him. As we'll see again in chapter 7, Jesus essentially says, *Do your worst; I have nothing to lose*.

Pilate retorts, "So you're a king!" He offers Jesus one last chance to retract his treachery and plead for pity. But Jesus is impenitent. His curt response cuts to the core of his kingdom's nonviolence:

> "In fact, the reason I was born and came into the world is to witness to the truth. Everyone on the side of truth listens to me." (John 18:37)

This is fire. *Truth* is king—not any human power. And truth's witness calls out for active *listening*—not coercion and killing like Pilate. Jesus daringly claims that this truth is embodied in his vision and practice of God's kingdom. The people who get where reality is going are willing to listen.

In this way, Jesus shifts the balance of power with the ruler of Jerusalem. He doesn't crumble as a victim or beg for mercy. He challenges Pilate to enter into dialogue and genuine listening. If Pilate refuses, the implication is that Pilate himself is a pawn of a violent kingdom that's actually passing away. Violence isn't a sign of strength but insecurity. The kingdom of heaven offers something better and stronger, even though it passes through suffering.

We'll finish this story in chapter six. The sixth movement of Jesus's prayer focuses on premeditated nonviolence, and we'll explore that in detail.

But what we'll find is that Jesus doesn't crumble. His embrace of his divine belovedness, his reverence for God's mystery, and his desire for the kingdom of heaven sustain him. He is unafraid and unconformed to religious hate and political violence. His moment of greatest pain breaks open into the promise of the kingdom for the criminal being executed beside him. The finality of death is overridden by heaven's rebellious hope.[23]

This ruggedly nonviolent witness is what we're signing up for when we pray with the criminalized and crucified Jesus, *Your kingdom come on earth as it is in heaven.*

Sign 5: Ordinary Work

The kingdom of heaven may courageously defy our world's rules. But it's meant for our world. Jesus teaches us to imagine, desire, and pray for its *coming—here on earth*—not our going somewhere else.

Jesus's spirituality is free of escapism and the numbing "religious opium" that Karl Marx rightly criticized.[24] As Thich Nhat Hanh wrote so beautifully about Jesus's prayerful life,

"We do not have to die to arrive at the gates of Heaven. In fact, we have to be truly alive. The practice is to touch life deeply so that the Kingdom of God becomes a reality."[25]

As we've seen, Jesus was trained as a carpenter, and he touched life deeply. Throughout his stories, Jesus describes how the kingdom grows through our ordinary work and everyday vocations on earth. He pictures it as a man planting a mustard seed in soil, which grows into a source of shelter for birds. He illustrates it with a woman kneading yeast into sixty pounds of dough, which rises up and nourishes the hungry (Matthew 13:31-32).

Jesus's stories of the kingdom dignify human labor. Whether carpentry, farming, baking, or another venture, they indicate that the kingdom shows up everywhere, through every kind of work, in ways that may initially appear insignificant. The seed gets swallowed in the soil; the yeast disappears into the dough. But this humble, hands-on work catalyzes an uprising as we pray for the kingdom to come on earth as it is in heaven.

The peace practitioner David Hartsough offers us a powerful example of what this can look like today.

Hartsough was a high school student in Virginia in the 1960s. At that time, white and Black students were forbidden from eating together under America's racist policy of segregation. Hartsough was a follower of Jesus, and so he refused to leave his lunch counter until African Americans were also allowed to eat there as equals. He celebrated God's new we—right where he was, in the way that he could.

After two days of sitting there, a white man pulled out a knife, put it to Hartsough's chest, and threatened to kill him. He sneered, "Well, n*****-lover, you have one minute to get out before I run this into your heart."

This man's privileged sense of superiority was threatened by a simple act of equity. He responded like the outraged bosses in

Jesus's story of the kingdom who complained, "You're making them equal to us!" Hartsough's basic desire to *eat* with his Black neighbors felt like intolerable treachery.

But Hartsough repeatedly practiced Jesus's prayer for the kingdom to come during these thirty-six hours of peacefully sitting in his school's cafeteria. So when the man insulted him and put the knife to his chest, Hartsough was prepared and untriggered. He calmly answered his potential killer, "Brother, you do what you feel you have to, but I'm going to try to love you no matter what."

Like Jesus before Pilate, Hartsough had the power to respond to violence with truth in love free of anger or aggression. He called God our Father, and so he considered Black people his family; he even called this violent racist *brother*. He hallowed G-d's name, and so he wasn't duped by a racist system propped up in the name of a white supremacist "God." He prayed for God's kingdom to come on earth, and so he acted in the small way that he could as a student in school.

The man was so shocked by this response that he eventually backed away, dropped the knife, and broke down in tears.[26]

Hartsough's courageous act of sitting down until space was created at the table for others to eat with dignity illustrates the way Jesus described the mysterious growth of the kingdom. It happened in everyday life, right where he already was, as a youth without any title or authority. In the moment, his risky action seemed small, inconsequential, and doomed to fail—hardly a sign of a "kingdom" that could overthrow American racism.

But this local act was part of a larger movement. And he and countless others like him—mostly courageous African Americans like Rosa Parks, Martin Luther King, and Thurgood Marshall—helped repeal a seemingly unchangeable legal system of dehumanization. It was Kingdom 101: countercultural love, mutual relationships, and integrated healing embodied through nonviolent witness and everyday action.

Refreshingly, Jesus never gives us a list of jobs or vocations that "best" serve the kingdom of heaven. As a carpenter himself, his examples typically come from blue-collar work. Whatever embodies the kingdom's values can serve the kingdom's coming— whether it looks like bagging groceries, painting gardens, working a kitchen, serving in hospitals, or dismantling an unjust legal system.

Dr. King eloquently articulated the kingdom's dignifying vision of human labor:

> "Whatever your life's work is, do it well... If it falls your lot to be a street sweeper, sweep streets like Michelangelo painted pictures, like Shakespeare wrote poetry, like Beethoven composed music... We have before us the glorious opportunity to inject a new dimension of love into the veins of our civilization."[27]

When we pray with Jesus for heaven's coming, we reorient and reroot ourselves in the earth. God's kingdom is for our precious planet, and we can all participate in its coming wherever we are in all that we say and do with love.

God's Dream

What do you want? Jesus asks us. What fills our imagination and fires our desire?

Jesus doesn't dream of skyscrapers and spaceships, as spectacular as they may be.

First, Jesus dreams of countercultural love that crosses boundaries to rediscover the sacred value of the most devalued people. This is the leap that takes us from history as we know it into heaven on earth. People are Peniel.

Second, Jesus reimagines human relationships so no one looks down while another looks up. The kingdom is where people stand face-to-face in mutuality.

Third, Jesus's desire burns for a holistic healing that reintegrates souls and bodies, persons and communities, heaven and earth. He's driven to restore home for the stigmatized and segregated.

Fourth, Jesus embodies nonviolent witness and refuses to mimic the imperial desire that unsuccessfully tried to end him. Truth and listening are how the kingdom comes—not torture and killing.

Fifth, Jesus mobilizes this dream with God's own Presence and our action. Each of us can participate in the coming of God's kingdom on earth—whoever we are, in all that we say and do, right here and right now.

When this divine dream unfurls in our imagination and ignites our desire, our flourishing is supercharged and opens into a new future. The kingdom of heaven isn't a replay of imperial pasts with their privilege and power. It's also not fuzzy feelings and happy thoughts for golden streets far off in a fake world. It's what W.H. Auden called "a paradigm now of what a plausible Future might be."[28] And this paradigm propels "loyal opposition" to the current order of things for something better—something God promises to complete when our cosmic endgame is fully realized.

When we bathe in God's love and disavow our false religion, this is what bursts out of us and becomes possible for our world. It's our Father's dream and our destiny, a personal and planetary purpose far more precious than the finest pearls. Sell everything, Jesus says, and invest all your stock into this everlasting venture.

But stopping here easily inflates into an overlofty spirituality. Humans are prone to messiah complexes. And this arrogant ambition easily metastasizes right back into our old imperial addictions— even as we imagine ourselves to be conquering "new worlds" for "God."[29] Empire always suppresses our basic needs and starves the empathy required for our embodied vulnerability.

So where Jesus takes us next is surprising and grounding, from the revolutionary right back to the ordinary—to the bread we eat and the question of what we really need to flourish.

There is more to practice.

Practice Flourishing

1. Take inventory of the "kingdoms" that shape your imagination, influence your desire, and ask for your loyalty. They may be religious or cultural groups, media platforms or websites, brands or corporations, educational institutions, political parties, governments, and/or other entities. You can usually identify them by the amount of your attention, emotion, time, money, and energy they demand. Make a list.

2. Review the five signs of the kingdom in Jesus's moral imagination: countercultural love, mutual relationships, integrated healing, nonviolent witness against injustice, and ordinary work.

3. In light of these values, reevaluate your relationship to each of the kingdoms on your list. Do they reflect and advance these values? Do they ignore or contradict them? Recommit to investing your imagination, desire, and practice into purposeful work that aligns with your values and welcomes the kingdom of heaven on earth.

Chapter 4

How Much Is Enough?
Our Daily Bread

A Practice of Subversive Simplicity

"Don't worry about tomorrow, because tomorrow's gonna worry about itself."
Jesus (Matthew 6:34)

"It is in exchanging the gifts of the earth that you shall find abundance and be satisfied. Yet unless the exchange be in love and kindly justice, it will but lead some to greed and others to hunger."
Khalil Gibran[1]

65

Just a Little Bit More

We're entering into the center of Jesus's prayer now, and we're reminded that humans are hungry creatures.

We're hungry for food, of course. But we're also hungry for *more*—for more stuff, more security, more success and status. Perhaps more often than we realize, we're hungry for surplus and a sense of superiority to others.

This hunger for more is hardwired into how we think about "kingdoms," why we fight for them, and why our world today is still plagued with human hunger. Ironically, praying for God's kingdom to come on earth may trigger these competitive cravings and make us feel entitled to them.

Jesus anticipates our addiction. And so with the fulcrum of his prayer, he presciently pivots us from praying for the kingdom to praying for our daily bread. Lest we inflate our egos and fly off on another power trip, Jesus immediately reroots us in our basic needs and embodied vulnerabilities on earth.

The question humming here is simple but challenging and vital to our flourishing: *How much is enough?*

The first American billionaire John D. Rockefeller was asked how much was enough for him. Rockefeller came from a poor family, but he went on to become the wealthiest person in modern history. He single-handedly founded my alma mater, the University of Chicago, with its soaring Rockefeller Memorial Chapel and castle-like campus. The story goes that Rockefeller answered, "Just a little bit more."[2]

These words capture the seemingly insatiable nature of human desire and the addictive spirit of consumerism.

Consumer culture is engineered to trigger our craving for "more" through constant messages and images. These signals incessantly work to sculpt our imagination and trigger our desire. Their goal is to make us feel and believe—often unconsciously—that if we just had a little bit *more*, we'd be happier and healthier, more attractive and influential—more beloved and established in our kingdom. The sales pitch to us "happiness machines" is simple but extremely powerful: me + more = flourishing.[3]

With this seductive promise, consumerism programs us to compare ourselves with others: *What do they have that I or we don't?* We begin measuring our worth with competition and a gnawing sense of scarcity—of something *more* that we need to be *enough*. Competition fuels pride, envy, and insecurity. And these incendiary emotions ignite conflict, just like the patriarchal system of privilege and resentment that Jesus disavowed when he taught us to call God *our* Father.

So how much is really enough if G-d is our loving Parent and God's kingdom is truly our heart's desire?

Simply asking this question is already an act of cultural nonconformity. It interrupts the sovereign assumption that more is always better and that our lives should be driven by a restless search for something else. Of course, this "something else" may be money, a feeling, an accomplishment, a status, a place, a person, or... more.

And here we uncover one of the most dangerous symptoms of our addiction to consumerism. Creaturely life and the earth itself become objects to own instead of opportunities for wonder. People get thingified into objects to possess rather than neighbors to love. We see again and again that consumerism desecrates and discards the God-facing Peniels that Jesus says are most precious to the kingdom. This is how the beloved of heaven become the wretched of the earth.

This is why clarifying what's enough for us is so crucial. When we know how much is enough, we can finally rest. Comparison, competition, and conflict are cut off. Endless craving no longer controls us. We learn to live conscious rather than *consumed* lives.

And so we harness our hunger and rediscover a healthy appetite for what is truly enough for our flourishing. And then, this enoughness nourishes us to turn outward. People who know how much is enough can foster empathy for our neighbors who need food, water, clothing, welcome, healthcare, and justice—the basics that Jesus mentions in his climactic story of the kingdom.

How much is enough? With subversive simplicity, Jesus teaches us to pray, *Give us today our daily bread* (Matthew 6:11; Luke 11:3).[4] We can take daily bread to mean our basic needs like food, water, shelter, healthcare, and security. For Jesus, our daily bread is enough. It's the right metric for rescaling our desire and what we rightly request from God every day. It's what we need to serve God's kingdom. When we have our daily bread, our Father has generously provided enough for us, and hearty gratitude is the fitting mindset.

There's much insight for practicing a flourishing life kneaded into Jesus's prayer for our daily bread. It brings together at least three dimensions that I'll explore in this chapter: first, trust that God actually cares about our basic needs; second, interdependence on the G-d who doesn't promise us surplus or invulnerable security; and third, empathy for others who also experience hunger and vulnerability.

Bread: The Courageous Mother Who Taught Me to Trust God for Our Needs

In his previous movement of prayer, Jesus responded to one of humanity's burning questions: *What do you want?* As we've seen, Jesus taught us to pray for God's kingdom—God's dream—to come on earth as it is in heaven.

After such an exalted petition, pivoting to pray for our daily bread may seem unimportant or even offensive to "God." Shouldn't we be ashamed to talk to our hallowed G-d about our hungry needs, our embodied appetites, and anxieties?

But Jesus takes us back to where his spirituality begins. God is our Father. And our Father opens the kingdom to us when we have nothing, calls us beloved, and cares about our basic needs. These things aren't small or insignificant to the God who numbers our hair.

So suppressing our rumbling stomachs and anxious hearts isn't actually spiritual. It's a denial—whether fearful or prideful—of who God is as our Parent and who we are as God's beloved children. Daily bread locks into Jesus's prayer for the kingdom to come on *earth* as it is in heaven.

We see God's concern for our physical needs in Jesus's personal practice.

Not long after launching his movement, Jesus sends his students off on their first independent mission of "proclaiming the kingdom of God and healing the sick." When they return, they ecstatically report to Jesus their amazing accomplishments. Interestingly, Jesus doesn't tell them to accelerate, scale up, and do more. Instead, Jesus recognizes that they need rest, and together they "withdraw" to a remote village (Luke 9:2, 10).

But the crowds crash their retreat, and Jesus doesn't turn them away. Instead, Jesus responds by "welcoming them, speaking to them about the kingdom of God, and healing those who needed healing." Here we see the signs of chapter three: love, relationship, and healing. Jesus spends time with these retreat-crashers until "late in the afternoon" (Luke 9:11).

The response of Jesus's closest students is striking. They feel like they've finished the important work of preaching the kingdom and healing the suffering. So they tell Jesus to send the people away to look for food and shelter on their own.

But Jesus's love is like his Father's. Jesus's biographer tells us that "he had compassion" for these people, and he refuses to send them away hungry. Instead, he challenges his kingdom-proclaiming, miracle-performing practitioners, "*You* give them something to eat" (Matthew 14:14; Luke 9:13). Recall Jesus's warning that many people say, "Lord! Lord!" but resist doing the will of our Father in heaven.

Still, the disciples protest that they don't have enough and that "spending that much on bread" would be an enormous waste of money. Ironically, the disciples had just depended on the generous hospitality of others as they traveled around Palestine proclaiming the kingdom and healing the sick. But like so many of us, they took this hospitality for granted and didn't see it as *itself* a vital embodiment of God's kingdom. For them, the important work was done, and they didn't care if people were hungry.

What follows is one of Jesus's most beautiful miracles.

He tells his students to bring the small amount of food that they actually have. Jesus holds it in his hands, looks up to heaven, and thanks God for it. Here again we see the reintegration of heaven and earth: Jesus holds bread, raises his grateful consciousness to the source of his belovedness, and prays with trust in a moment of scarcity. Then Jesus tells his students to start distributing the food to the crowd.

I can almost imagine holding a few scraps of bread in my hands and walking into a crowd of thousands of hungry people. A feeling of powerlessness and embarrassment flares up within me. But this is what they do, and in the end, "they all ate and were satisfied." Ironically enough, there were twelve basketfuls of leftovers—one for each of Jesus's anxious followers (Luke 9:16-17).

This miracle remains deliciously mysterious. Did Jesus himself turn five loaves and two fish into a meal that fed around ten thousand hungry people? Or did Jesus's compassionate risk of sharing his food inspire people in the crowd to share what they had brought for themselves—and together they already had *enough for everyone*?

In either case, what matters to us is that food mattered to Jesus. In fact, soon after, Jesus did the exact same thing for a slightly smaller crowd, making sure that everyone had enough to eat (Matthew 15:32).

There's challenging hope here for all of us.

Like many of us today, Jesus's students still hadn't internalized that the kingdom belongs to our Father and that our Father cares for our basic embodied needs. They dismissed daily bread as unspiritual and didn't mind if people went hungry.

But for Jesus, sharing food is just as important as proclaiming the kingdom and healing the sick. In fact, it's an embodiment of the kingdom's presence, and he insists on people being fed.

So Jesus teaches us to bluntly and boldly ask God, *Give us today our daily bread*. This isn't unspiritual. It's the most basic way of confessing that we actually trust that God is who Jesus says God is: our Parent who listens to our prayers and cares for our needs.

When I was a pastor in Ethiopia, I committed to walking to work for six months. This daily walk took me through the heart of Addis's shiny economic development. And yet on Africa Avenue, amidst the new shopping malls and stuffed grocery stores, there were numerous street children begging for bread. My heart was broken seeing small kids the same age as my beloved nieces and nephews out on the streets, late into the night, hungry for food.

So I decided to save my bus money, walk on foot, and buy meals for the kids on my way home from work at night. This wasn't about virtue signaling or being a white savior in Africa. I wanted to meet these children right where they were and cultivate the face-to-face relationship that Jesus says brings heaven to earth. It wasn't much, but it's what I could do rooted in my everyday practice.

The beautiful smiles that erupted on these children's faces continue to glow in my memory through the years. They were intimately familiar with hunger and humiliation, with want and being unwanted. For a stranger to approach them with love and *food* was a source of joy and thanksgiving. Our simple meals were like tiny foretastes of the kingdom's global party breaking out right there on Africa Avenue.

These impoverished children became my professors of radical trust in God. They helped me digest in the core of my being that our bodily health and sharing bread are just as important to God as anything we can ever do in a church building.

Wudenesh was one of the little girls that I met on the street during those walks. She had deep, kind eyes and walked with a clanky cane due to her bone tuberculosis. After sharing several meals, Wudenesh led me to her home deep in a nearby slum and introduced me to her strong mother Itash and the rest of her family.

For over a decade now, I've often sat in Itash's mud-walled, one-room home and listened to her talk about trusting God as we eat her delicious injera—Ethiopia's daily bread. Itash and Wudenesh graced Lily and me as our guests of honor at our engagement party. We've celebrated many joyful holidays and birthdays together ever since.

Through the years, I've always taken my ethics students for a meal at Itash's humble home. This is our most important classroom, and this courageous woman serves as one of our prophetic professors. She always tells us, "If I have just one cup of coffee per day, I give thanks to God." In the midst of her joys and struggles, Itash resiliently embodies trust in God and gratitude for daily bread.

Her example has profoundly challenged me to reimagine the meaning of enough.[5]

Daily: Eyob's Story of Absolute Dependence

Itash's words point to the next insight of Jesus's response to *How much is enough?* Here we see that God challenges our craving for surplus and invulnerable security by only promising us our *daily* bread. Jesus's second practice of hallowing G-d comes back to the center, reminding us of God's mysterious otherness.

With this prayer, Jesus is alluding to the story where God tests Israel's craving for more and requires daily dependence. After Moses encounters I-Shall-Be at the burning bush and leads the Hebrew slaves into liberation, the story continues:

> "And the Lord said to Moses, 'Look, I am about to rain down bread for you from the heavens, and the people shall go out and gather *each day's* share on *that day*, so that I may test them whether they will go by My Teaching or not."[6] (Exodus 16:4, emphasis added)

These people had just been emancipated from 400 years of slavery, and God's kingdom was finally coming on earth for them with freedom, dignity, and hope. But now they find themselves wandering in a barren desert—hungry and ironically craving the food of Egypt. Of course, Egypt was filled with misery and suffering. But its oppressive regiment was also *certain* and *secure*.

The unknown is powerfully unnerving. We often have a higher tolerance for enslavement than uncertainty. We'd rather survive oppression than embrace the vulnerable liberation of depending on an invisible God and walking forward in freedom.

So God designs a test to help these traumatized people continue emancipating themselves from the Egyptian empire's enslaving pseudo-security. G-d promises to miraculously *rain* bread from heaven, indicating the abundance of God's storehouse. But God instructs the people to gather only enough for *each day*. This daily rhythm was designed to foster dependence on God to provide again tomorrow—or to expose that they secretly worshiped material surplus and the false security it promises.

Understandably, many of these recently liberated people didn't accept that daily bread was truly enough. Hebrew poems reflect back on this challenging experience and opine,

> "They soon forgot God's deeds; they wouldn't wait to learn
> His plan. They were seized with craving in the wilderness."
> (Psalm 106:13-14)

And so, forgetful of the past and anxious for the future, they go out in the morning and stockpile as much bread as they can carry, questioning, "Can God spread a feast in the wilderness?" (Psalm 78:19).[7]

But their backup plan backfires. Their stockpile spoils by the day's end, and having more doesn't satisfy their anxiety or secure their future. And so they face a sobering recognition: even after an extraordinary experience of God's kingdom coming on earth to the point of freedom from slavery, they still didn't really depend on God. They doubted that God is our Father who loves us as precious children and can be depended upon to meet our daily needs.

I identify with the Israelites. Daily bread ignites my anxiety and doesn't satisfy my craving for surplus and security—for monthly or yearly, or even lifetime bread. In fact, it sets on my table unsettling facts that we all know but so often suppress.

First, we can't know or control tomorrow or really even the next moment.

Second, this means that we're fundamentally vulnerable, dependent creatures.

And, third, this means that the unknown tomorrow is haunted by the shadow of death itself. No matter how much bread we stockpile—even Rockefeller's fortune—we're neither self-sufficient nor exempted from our own mortality. Whether today, tomorrow, or off into the unknowable future, we will all die and face that ultimate test of absolute dependence on God for our life.[8]

So daily bread provokes these gut-checking, often gut-wrenching questions: Can we live mindfully with contentment in the present when the future is uncertain? Are we willing to choose a life of absolute dependence on God so we can take risks for God's kingdom? Are we getting ready to let go of our lives and fall into the hands of the Father who promises to welcome us home into the feast of heaven's global party? Or do we still believe in our anxious guts that *our* kingdom ultimately sustains us and that having *more* is the key to our flourishing?

When I was finishing my PhD at Rockefeller's University of Chicago, Lily and I felt strongly that God wanted us to take a risk. We discerned a call to return to our beloved Ethiopia and continue serving God's kingdom there for free.

In the years before my program, I had worked as a volunteer pastor on a tiny budget, as I mentioned above, and I didn't have any savings. Lily and I got married in an Ethiopian government office housed in a metal storage container. Tom, the director of USAID in Ethiopia, wryly joked, "You literally shacked up!" We then moved back to Chicago very much in love but without money, and our income was just enough to cover our basic needs during those stressful years.

When we were praying about moving back to Ethiopia, we still didn't have any savings. And the Ethiopian Graduate School of Theology where I agreed to teach couldn't offer me a salary. The call was clear, but the path was entirely uncertain.

As our move got closer, I vividly remember washing the dishes after dinner one night and praying at the sink like Brother Lawrence: *Give us today our daily bread*. I could feel my stomach churning inside me with nauseous anxiety. My mind was wracked with questions that I couldn't answer, and my body surged with the fear of our uncertain future: *What if we sell everything, move to Ethiopia, and fall flat on our faces? What if I can't provide for Lily, our marriage falls apart, and our lives are filled with unbearable pain?* Lily came from a low-income family in Addis, and the thought of subjecting her to more scarcity was crushing to me. The inner voice screamed at me, "What an irresponsible husband!"

Praying with Jesus for our daily bread felt more like a distressing prelude to disaster than a practice of flourishing.

Then January 4th came—Lily's and my unexpected Independence Day.

I had recently graduated from UChicago, and that morning I spent several hours wrestling with Jesus's prayer like Jacob's unnamed Stranger at Peniel. I needed to knead it into my soul—to *practice* it over and over again like I did those thousand shots on that cement slab of my youth. The repetition wasn't for God to hear me but for the meaning of the words to sink into my anxious soul.

When I finished praying, I checked my email and saw a message at the top of my inbox from Joelle. As I read her words, I was shocked and blown away. She asked if her family could cover half of our budget for several years of service in Ethiopia. Who *asks* if they can give you their money?!

I had only recently met Joelle over coffee on UChicago's campus through Jenna, her daughter and one of my most brilliant students. After I walked home from our meeting, I wasn't expecting anything like this. But Joelle wrote that they were passionate about "risky startup work" and were compelled by our vision.

Lily and I could hardly believe her email was real. It felt like a huge mountain blocking our path had been leveled right before our eyes and we literally danced for joy in our apartment that afternoon. We called it our "eucatastrophe"—Tolkien's word for something so good that it's *catastrophically* good.

But our Independence Day wasn't over. That night I watched Eyob's final video message for the first time.

Eyob—Amharic for Job—was a skinny 13-year-old boy that I had met on the streets of Addis fifteen years before. Our paths crossed unexpectedly soon before I started my PhD in Chicago.

On May 1st, I was sitting at a streetside cafe with friends. Eyob approached our table and begged us to help him. But a waiter arrived with our daily bread, and we said no to his request. As Eyob turned to walk away, his soiled hood slipped off his head, and I saw a horrifying wound that looked like an oozing crater on the back of his skull.

I soon found out that Eyob had fallen into a cooking fire as a small child. His family was poor, and he never got the urgent medical care that he needed from that day on and for the rest of his childhood. Through the years, his burn wound got so bad that his parents sent him to Addis on a pickup truck to beg for help or to die.

By the time we met on the street that day, I could see Eyob's brain pulsing through his wound. I had never witnessed anything so hideous—so unbearably painful and so violently warring against human dignity and this boy's very being. His wound struck me like a refutation of everything good and all that brings joy. Tears overflow in my eyes as I write these words and remember Eyob's wounded head still now like yesterday.

I warred within myself: *Should I get up and help this kid, or eat my lunch with my friends and hope for the best?* As Eyob walked away, I heard the Voice out of Jesus's final story about "the least of these," the end of the world, and our ultimate hope in the kingdom of heaven. The Voice told me, *Andrew, if you say no to him, you've said no to me.* And I knew immediately what I needed to do.

My friends and I spent the next several months fighting for Eyob's precious life in a local hospital. Eyob and I shared many days together in the burn ward, and I discovered him to be anything but a refutation of goodness and joy.

Eyob was Peniel—God's Face for me. He was kind, funny, courageously loving, and generously giving. I keep a picture of him on my desk in which he pointed to a piece of paper on the hospital's wall that said, "God is Love." Whenever we'd bring him presents or his favorite foods, he'd immediately start sharing everything with the other children in the beds beside his. He embodied absolute dependence on the loving enoughness of God in a way that I have never experienced before or since then.

Against my deepest fears, Eyob convinced me that we are not abandoned or alone. We are all the beloved children of God, and when we suffer, God suffers with us. The King of heaven's kingdom is with the least of these. Somehow, in ways I still don't fully understand but am learning to trust, God's unseen hands hold us safely when life crucifies us like it did Eyob.

Eyob became my saint of darkness, an incarnation of Jesus's climactic story about our world's ultimate endgame. He was an outsider with nothing but the filthy clothes on his back and excruciating pain in his body. And yet he was so closely connected to the joy and hope of heaven. His surgeries required him to wear white bandages on his head, and we mirthfully called him our *shemagele*, because he hilariously looked like a traditional Ethiopian elder wearing a white turban. He was a boy who embodied the mature flourishing of an entire lifetime.

But our best efforts couldn't bring the kingdom's healing for Eyob. Apparently, he was sent to bring it to us and receive his healing in heaven. After several surgeries and grueling skin grafts, the tests came back, and we found out that Eyob had terminal brain cancer. Nothing more could be done to save his life.

Lily and I invited Eyob to be the guest of honor at our small wedding party soon before we moved to Chicago. At the end of the night, I'll never forget how Eyob hugged me once more in the street and the last words that he spoke to me: *Andrew, may God be with you always*.

My friends helped Eyob return home to his family in the countryside, and he died a few months later. But soon before, Eyob recorded a final message for Lily and me on a friend's phone.

Providentially, my friend forgot to send us the video, and I saw it for the first time five years later—on January 4th. It was that eucatastrophic day on which I received Joelle's email, shortly after I had held Eyob's picture pointing to "God is Love" over my heart as I graduated from the University of Chicago and fearfully faced our unknown future.

Somehow in G-d's holy mystery, this massive delay was perfectly on time.

It still brings tears to my eyes to remember this hallowed moment. Eyob sat on the floor in a small room like Itash's house. He was still wearing the white, turban-like bandages on his head. And he spoke into the camera with his gentle yet convicted voice and face full of love:

> "My dear brother Andrew, whom I love more than anything, and my sister Lily, we are one in Jesus. Be strong and work hard, and God will be with you and support you! Till you go to heaven—till you receive the reward from the hand of God—be strong and serve God intensely. May peace be with you."

I was shattered—flooded with love and loss, joy and grief, missing and hope for Eyob. A river flowed from my eyes as heaven opened and I was engulfed in our divine belovedness.

Eyob then spoke to us with the words of the Prophet Isaiah. He quoted from memory,

> "I will go before you and level the mountains;
> I will break down gates of bronze and cut through bars of iron.
> I will give you hidden treasures, riches stored in secret places,
> so that you may know that I am the Lord who calls you by name."
> (Isaiah 45:2-3)

As I listened to these holy words, it felt like Eyob was speaking to me straight from heaven beyond death itself—out of time and yet so entirely in time. He prophesied to this precise day in my life. This was the day when I was surging with anxiety, wrestling with Jesus's prayer, and dancing for joy over a mountain that had been leveled by our friends' promise of their hidden treasures. It was like Eyob knew that Joelle's family was coming—five years before I had even met them. And he was certain that we would be okay. *Be strong and serve God intensely.*

Eyob's voice reverberated in my heart, and my past and future folded together in trust like a sacred map. In the background of Eyob's message, I could faintly hear singing from a nearby church, which rejoiced, "The redemption of the world! The redemption of the world! Praise be to you, Jesus! The redemption of the world!"

Heaven opened and that river of divine belovedness flowed through me with safety, healing, and hope. I was certain that Eyob was well and that I no longer needed to fear taking this risk of returning to Ethiopia.

Of course, Eyob had known terrible suffering from his earliest memories to the end of his earthly life. Daily bread was all he ever had—and often didn't have. And yet Eyob had become a prophetic witness—in his life and from heaven long after his death—that God can be depended upon absolutely and will always meet our needs.

With Eyob as our founder, we sold everything, moved to Ethiopia, and never lacked anything. In the years that followed, we built the Neighbor-Love Movement with the mission of lifting up the dignity of other Peniels like Eyob.[9]

As I look back on Lily's and my journey, I'm grateful for that intensely anxious chapter in our life and how it lingers with us today. We face death threats for our work amidst Ethiopia's devastating civil war and remain intimately familiar with uncertainty. I'll share some of that story in chapter six.

But we continue to witness that our Father loves us and cares about our basic needs, even when surplus and security aren't part of the package. Praying with Jesus for daily bread is rescaling our desires and liberating us to depend on God absolutely, like Eyob, with our own uncertainty, vulnerability, and death.

Somehow, *daily* bread is actually *enough*, and we can depend on it—now and always.

Our: Empathy to End Hunger

Finally, notice that Jesus teaches us to pray for *our* daily bread.

Just like Jesus invites us to call God *our* Father, Jesus reminds us that *our* hunger is shared when we truly practice flourishing. And the result is profound. That most intimate and unsettling experience of anxious insecurity in the pit of our stomachs can become a womb of stretching empathy with others.[10]

Of course, the opposite is often true. When we feel vulnerable and like we scarcely have enough, we're easily engulfed in our distress. Anger and fear bubble up inside. As we saw in Nazi Germany, we're tempted to isolate or become aggressive. We convince ourselves that we don't have any extra for the anxieties of others.

But Jesus's prayerful practice pries open our private property. When we pray for *our* daily bread, we're reminded daily that others also hunger. Others also know the anxiety of insecurity. Others also fear that they're on the brink of falling apart. Others are also triggered to isolate or attack when they feel like enough is impossible.

We need to recall the *we* that Jesus is invoking with his prayer for *our* daily bread. The people who first prayed with Jesus were from every part of Palestine, locals and foreigners. They were people in severe pain, with mental illness and physical disabilities. They were people who knew stigma and exclusion—people who likely saw each other with suspicion and enmity.

But Jesus teaches them to pray for our daily bread as if they're eating from a single loaf at a shared table. We're not alone in our embodied needs and vulnerabilities. When we practice flourishing with Jesus, we are truly *companions*, neighbors who learn to break bread with one another.[11] And what so easily produces isolation and conflict undergoes a *metanoia* that can produce empathy and a sustaining interdependence.

This points back again to the fierce tenderness of *our* Father in chapter one. Our Father loves and liberates all of us as beloved children, guards the vulnerable, and desires none to be destroyed. If we're truly praying to the Father who holds all of us, only asking for *my* bread or *my group's* bread doesn't make any sense. That is never enough.

So whether we can pray and work for *our* daily bread tests whether we hallow G-d's name or grasp for a hollow "God" that's just an individualistic coping mechanism or tribal trump card. This prayer also tests whether we've made the kingdom's countercultural VIP list our passion, or whether we're still struggling for a kingdom that defaces and starves our world's Peniels.

In this way, Jesus's prayer for our daily bread sounds the alarm against the devastating evil of human hunger still today. It denounces the scourge of food insecurity that is unleashed by hungry human kingdoms and their wars, which prevent fields from being sown, destroy harvests, and starve our sacred siblings. We cannot pray with Jesus's G-d and tolerate the rapacious violence that makes answering his prayer for our daily bread impossible.[12]

With the fulcrum of his spiritual practice, then, Jesus subtly reprograms our prayers for "more" into prayerful empathy with and for real people who are actually praying for their daily bread. This is the meal of the day laborer, the minimum-wage worker, the families without savings or insurance, the children in our streets, and the victims of our wars.

Prayerful consciousness is unshackled from consumerism, and we attune ourselves to the vulnerability and suffering of our neighbors. We suddenly hear the muffled rumbling of empty stomachs to which we would have remained deaf without this prayer. And with practice, our tables begin to be shared with rebellious empathy and interdependence in the kingdom of God across our borders. These shared tables—at home and in halls of power—become birthplaces for new programs and policies for our shared flourishing.

This is exactly what we witness in Jesus's movement soon after he sends his followers out across all the boundaries of the empire. From the start, Jesus's practitioners organized a "daily distribution of food" for impoverished women in the community. In fact, they empowered ethnic minority communities to elect their own leaders to ensure that the distribution of daily bread was equitable for all. This is one of the first examples of genuinely egalitarian democracy in history.[13] (Greek democracy is far more famous, but it only allowed wealthy, land-owning men to vote. Women and those without property—the people at the center of attention in Acts 6:1-7—were excluded.)

For the first followers of Jesus, daily bread wasn't only a pious prayer. It was a practical policy and program that met the physical needs of the most vulnerable.

This groundbreaking practice ended up revolutionizing care for impoverished and oppressed people in the Roman Empire. The early centuries of Jesus's movement innovated the first public hospitals, schools, orphanages, and nursing homes. The suffering of the Peniels who needed these services was finally recognized as important. Their boundary-breaking empathy started changing the world.[14]

Jesus's vision of our daily bread continues to energize empathy and socio-economic development around the world today. When we pray with Jesus, we receive a daily reminder to feel the pain of others and to participate in this life-saving movement.[15]

Our Eucatastrophe

So how much is enough in our consumeristic age that incessantly insists that me + more = flourishing?

Jesus's answer is subversively simple. He invites us to practice praying to our Father, *Give us today our daily bread*. Against our competitive cultures with their addictive ads and our gnawing anxiety, today's bread is enough for our flourishing.

First, our daily *bread* affirms that God actually cares for our physical needs. God isn't too exalted or God's kingdom too lofty to hear our prayer and provide for us as embodied creatures. Wudenesh and Itash are my professors of this resilient trust.

But, second, our *daily* bread challenges our craving for surplus and security. We learn that we don't need an endless supply to depend on God and take risks of faith. Eyob is my saint of darkness who collaborates with Jenna and Joelle's family in teaching me this absolute dependence.

Finally, *our* daily bread expands our empathy for the hunger of others. In doing so, it sets a shared table between us of mutual vulnerability and sustaining interdependence. As we pray, we innovate policies and programs that protect our shared flourishing and fight food insecurity, especially for our most vulnerable sacred siblings.

In the fulcrum of Jesus's prayer, we rediscover that we are fully beloved and that our flourishing will be fulfilled. Eyob is safe in heaven's kingdom. But Jesus's flourishing is fiercer than our hungry kingdoms. It leads us into a subversive simplicity that calls for our rebellious nonconformity. Authentic flourishing isn't driven by an endless craving for more that fuels our consumeristic, competitive culture of envy, pride, and conflict. True flourishing trusts in God and experiences a miracle: us + empathy = enough.

But reclining here easily drifts off into a dreamy denial of another troubling recognition: We hurt each other and often can't even sit at the same table. These painful conflicts drive us apart, mass-produce hunger, and cast doubt on whether a shared flourishing is really possible when the chips are down.

There is more to practice.

Practice Flourishing

When you plan your finances and discern your life's vocation, practice praying to our Parent, *Give us today our daily bread*. This prayer disrupts our addictions and cultivates four crucial virtues for our shared flourishing:

1. Gratitude for God's abundant provision.

2. Self-awareness when we're grasping for more than we need.

3. Empathy for the needs of others.

4. Courageous trust in our Father's "hidden treasures" when daily bread feels like it isn't enough to take risks for God's kingdom.

Chapter 5

How Do We Begin Again?
Forgive Us as We Forgive Others

A Practice of Courageous Healing

"This rigid refusal to look at ourselves may well destroy us…
The way to begin is by taking a hard look at oneself."[1]

James Baldwin

"Forgiveness is the possibility of a new start… The hardest words in any language are 'I'm sorry. Please forgive me,' and yet they alone can help restore a personal relationship which a wrong has disturbed."[2]

Desmond Tutu

A Troubling Recognition

We're entering into the second half of Jesus's prayer now, and he signals a subtle but significant transition here. The next three movements call for a new maturity that takes our flourishing into spiritual adulthood.[3]

Jesus moves from praying for our daily bread to facing the reality of our painful brokenness. He refuses to recline in the illusion that we share a cozy table with the kingdom coasting in. The reality is more difficult. We hurt each other and participate in what's wrong with the world. We are fallible creatures with painful conflicts and unfinished business.

This sobering reality casts a dark shadow over the first half of Jesus's prayer. Take a second look.

Our broken relationships degrade our confidence that God is a good Parent and that we are all beloved children in God's new we.

Our exploitative invocations of "God" desecrate G-d's name and sow suspicion that "God" is just a dangerous tool of deception and destruction.

Our competitive kingdoms clash and attack our faith that God's kingdom is actually coming and that our future can be trusted with hope.

Our excess and indifference to others' suffering leave us hungry and questioning whether we can ever be truly full.

Denial is an addictive defense mechanism that we use to deal with this distress. The psychologist Christopher Bollas writes, "Each of us is aware in ourselves of the workings of denial, of our need to be innocent of a troubling recognition."[4] Bollas's insight is compact and profound.

What he means is that we cling to our innocence out of our need to protect our fragile belief that we're good and worthy of love. This legitimate need for self-esteem often drives us to hide from our failures and to pretend like our problems aren't real. All too easily, we end up offloading our shame onto others by blaming them and entrenching ourselves in self-righteousness.

But the outcome is usually more pain and conflict. We refuse to know what we know about ourselves, and dishonesty creeps in. We grow apart, and resentment festers in the fraught space between us. The social fabric of our community comes undone, and we question whether a new future is really possible. "What a marvelous wreck we are," writes Amanda Gorman.[5]

So here in the second of half of Jesus's prayer, we face that urgent but unsettling question: *How do we begin again?*

The Discoverer of Forgiveness

Jesus's answer is forgiveness.

And so he teaches us to pray, *Forgive us for our sins as we forgive others who sin against us* (Matthew 6:12; Luke 11:4).[6] This sounds simple enough, but it's almost always challenging. This practice calls us into three crucial movements of healing that require enormous courage.

First, we need to face our failures head-on rather than hiding from what scares us. As Gorman writes, "Sometimes, we must call our monster out from under the bed to see that he/she/it carries our face."[7]

Second, we need to come clean and honestly confess these failures to God. As we do so, we don't wallow in guilt but learn to accept that God accepts us and wants to forgive us. Our failure is not the end of our story but an invitation to begin again.

And, third, we need to share this divine forgiveness with others who have hurt us. For Jesus, authentic forgiveness is always shared, or it remains a false start. When we practice forgiveness, polarization is undone, collective responsibility is born, and seemingly impossible futures of hope are unlocked.

Hannah Arendt called Jesus "the discoverer of forgiveness," and neuroscientists and psychiatrists have collected the empirical data that demonstrate just how important forgiveness truly is for our flourishing.[8]

For example, enjoying healthy relationships on a daily basis generates the same happiness that comes from an annual income boost of $100,000. Conversely, broken relationships increase our "risk of premature death from all causes by 50 percent." They produce negative health outcomes "equivalent to smoking fifteen cigarettes a day."[9] In *The Body Keeps the Score*, Bessel van der Kolk writes, "More than anything else, being able to feel safe with other people is probably the single most important aspect of mental health; safe connections are fundamental to meaningful and satisfying lives."[10]

Based on this data, the psychiatrist Curt Thompson concludes, "Confession and forgiveness may be the way to create more flexible, adaptive, coherent, energized, and stable individual minds and, by extension, communities that reflect the same qualities."[11]

Jesus's fifth movement of prayer, then, invites us to unsuppress our troubling recognitions. It unlocks denial and reconciles our relationships. It depolarizes people, deescalates conflict, and opens the way for making new beginnings. It's a courageous practice of healing that unhostages our flourishing.

What Is Forgiveness and Why Does It Matter?

Forgiveness is the choice to release others from their failure and to affirm their sacred value as siblings in God's family. The Greek verb that Jesus uses here—*aphiemi*—simply means to "let go" or "release." When we say, "I forgive you," we're really saying, "I hold on to you and let go of the pain you've caused me." Likewise, saying, "Please forgive me" means, "Hold on to me and release the pain I've caused you." Forgiveness courageously prioritizes people over pain.[12]

This is why forgiveness matters. It's the power of new beginning after we've ruptured our relationships. It unlocks the prison of the past and opens a fresh future. It suspends the ironclad law of cause and effect—of wrongdoing hammered by retribution. And so it gives birth to a miracle of newness in history: grace. It's a daily practice of unhostaging one another, of canceling debts and sharing undeserved moral generosity to start over. As bell hooks wrote, "Only love can heal the wounds of the past."[13]

But we know how difficult the process of forgiveness often is. When we harm one another, this failure can easily seem to define us or even exhaust who we are—whether as individuals or members of a group. Shame, anger, and revenge burn inside and between us like corrosive acids. We see the offender as simply too guilty and too worthy of rejection to be set free. When our pain is severe and our trauma unhealed, we may even see "them" as irredeemable and worthless—as anything but siblings in God's new we.

Before we know it, the ones who harmed us become the "other," people that we see as unrelated or less than ourselves. We start imagining them as our enemy, as uniquely corrupt and perhaps even less than human. Images creep into our minds of the other as an animal, a cancer, a monster or demon. In his important book *On Inhumanity*, David Livingstone Smith writes, "given the right circumstances, virtually all of us are capable of slipping into the dehumanizing mindset, and committing acts of cruelty that would otherwise be difficult or even impossible for us to perform."[14]

Smith is right. History repeatedly teaches us—or fails to teach us—that the othering mindset is the gateway to genocidal hate and hell on earth.[15]

The power of pain and the complexity of our emotions, then, show us what a challenging process and courageous choice forgiveness truly is. We so easily and understandably choose the opposite; we hold on to our pain and reject people.

Nelson Mandela called South Africa's White supremacist system of apartheid "the very embodiment of injustice."[16] But Desmond Tutu, Mandela's partner in South Africa's Truth and Reconciliation Commission, named what's at stake in this challenging choice: "without forgiveness, without reconciliation, we have no future."[17]

So Jesus's fifth practice takes us back to our beginnings and tests whether we truly trust them. Do we believe that God's love is primal and that everything real and enduring starts in our divine belovedness—to the point of forgiving people who have hurt us and perpetrated injustice? Or do we believe that evil is original and that we're hopelessly locked in a bitter struggle for survival that depends on eliminating the enemy?

The beginning we trust defines the horizon of our future.

God Wants to Forgive Us

As we've seen, Jesus's spirituality is anchored in this primal origin of divine love. God is our loving Parent, and we are we—God's beloved children. And so Jesus's fifth movement requires us to reimmerse ourselves in the divine baptism of his first.

Recall that Jesus describes God as "kind to the ungrateful and the wicked." Against popular religious visions, Jesus reintroduces us to God as the Lover of enemies. This divine vision inspired Jesus's beautiful story about the scandalously merciful father who runs to his disgraced son, hugging and kissing him as he welcomes him home after total failure. When the son confesses, "I am no longer worthy to be called your child," the father silences his shame and says, "Let's have a feast and celebrate!" (Luke 6:35-36; 15:23).

This vision of God is why Jesus teaches that God *wants* to *forgive us* rather than punishing and rejecting us when we fail. Before anyone else, God is that courageous Agent who chooses to hold on to us and release the pain we've caused. God is the infinitely creative Author who desires to start rewriting our story with redemption and hope.

Of course, our hallowed G-d holds us accountable. We need to recall Isaiah's response when he heard heavenly beings thunder, "Holy! Holy! Holy!" He cried out, "Woe to me! I am lost!" He faced his troubling recognition and immediately confessed his and his people's corruption. Like Jacob, the divine Stranger wrestles with us and refuses to be manipulated into our self-indulging puppet or cynical sin insurance card. We need to confess our failure.

But God *wants* to forgive us. God longs for us to experience that "safe connection" that van der Kolk calls "the single most important aspect of mental health."

The most dramatic example of this unconditional divine desire is Jesus's dying breath. Jesus's followers had abandoned him. Religious leaders, government authorities, and the crowds joined together into a jeering chorus that mocked his powerlessness. Jesus had seemingly lost everything except the shattering pain surging through his dying body.

And yet, Jesus doesn't invoke God's just judgment or damn them to hell. He cries out, "Father, *forgive* them for they don't know what they're doing." Jesus lets go of his excruciating pain and holds on to these murderously misguided people. In this way, God's mercy absorbs and overcomes violence, and the cycle of retribution is broken for our salvation (Luke 23:34).

If God can forgive Jesus's killers, who can't God forgive?[18]

And so Jesus invites us to confidently ask our Father to forgive our sins, just like we ask for our daily bread. No matter what we've done or how bad it's gotten, we don't need to be imprisoned in our past or consumed with guilt. That safe connection is still available to us. We can surrender our innocence, confront the voice that says, "You are no longer worthy!" and be set free to begin again as God's beloved children.

The greatest challenge here may be learning to forgive ourselves. The shame of what we've done or failed to do sticks to our insides like glue. The inner voice insists that we are unworthy of forgiveness and that our failure defines us. *Perhaps God forgives me,* we say. *But can I forgive and accept myself?*

We see afresh here how immersively bathing in our divine belovedness is essential to our healing and flourishing. We need to doubt our doubts and disbelieve the certainty of the voice that insists we're condemned and finished. The waters of our divine baptism are powerful and can wash away the poison of our self-rejection. The unconditional Voice from heaven interrupts shame's voice and declares, "I forgive you; you are my beloved child, and I still delight in you." With time, this heavenly Voice can come inside, and we can learn to accept that we're actually accepted.

With his healing hilarity, Desmond Tutu tells a clever parable of a man trapped in his shame. The man comes to God and says, "I'm sorry, I've done it again." But God asks, "What have you done?"

Tutu explains, "God suffers from amnesia when it comes to our sins. God does not look at the caterpillar we are now, but the dazzling butterfly we have it in us to become." Despite his acute familiarity with human evil, Tutu concludes,

> "There is nothing you can do that will make God love you less. There is nothing you can do to make God love you more. God's love for you is infinite, perfect, and eternal."[19]

This unrelenting forgiveness is how fiercely committed God is to our flourishing. According to Jesus, all we need to do is honestly ask—and *it's finished* (John 19:30).

We Can't Be Forgiven Alone

Nevertheless, Jesus never drifts away from his social vision of God. God is *our* Father, and that means that we can't be forgiven alone. For Jesus, there's simply no private pipeline to God. If we shut off forgiveness for others, we've shut it off for ourselves as well.

Seeking forgiveness without sharing it unmasks that we're still grasping for spiritual privilege from a tribal Patriarch in the sky. We haven't truly undergone the *metanoia* of our Father who invites us into God's new we. As Howard Thurman wrote, "Man's relation to man and man's relation to God are one relation. A death blow is struck to hypocrisy."[20]

Strikingly, this is the only part of Jesus's prayer that he unpacks with immediate commentary. Apparently, Jesus considered the practice of forgiveness to be so fundamental that he refuses to let us skate over it or misunderstand what's at stake. He wants it to interrupt and rewire our imagination, desire, and practice. So Jesus says,

> "If you forgive other people when they sin against you, you
> guys' heavenly Father will also forgive you. But if you
> don't forgive others their sins, you guys' Father won't for-
> give your sins." (Matthew 6:14-15)

The plural yous, which I've translated for emphasis as "you guys," are important. They remind us of who God truly is: *our* Father and so the Father of those we refuse to forgive.

Making our forgiveness conditional on forgiving others, then, isn't cheap tit-for-tat. It's a practical test that reveals whether we actually believe that God is *God* and that we are *we. Our* Parent loves us and wants to liberate *all* of us in the healing kingdom of heaven.

Jesus's socially attentive vision of forgiveness may strike some of us as heretical. Popular religion has perfected a system in which our individual sins are dealt with in a private transaction with God, while our relationships with others are seen as separate business. But Jesus overrides our system and disruptively insists that being forgiven without forgiving others isn't an option that G-d offers. Our salvation is God's free gift, but it's social. It's shared from start to finish—or it remains a false start.

We shouldn't be surprised that Jesus taught that forgiving others makes or breaks a real connection with God. Jesus himself was badly wronged by all kinds of people. He knew the necessity of forgiveness because he himself had to forgive others. We've seen already that Jesus narrowly escaped a political massacre and lost his home as a child. He was quickly othered and demonized for his heretical teaching. And he ended up being arrested and condemned as a public enemy.

These traumatizing experiences made Jesus acutely familiar with the pain of human failure and the devastating effects of our cyclical conflicts. But rather than hardening him, they intimately attuned Jesus to the urgent importance of making new beginnings and practicing a flourishing that can survive in the conflicts of the real world.

Unsurprisingly, then, Jesus elevated forgiving others even above traditional religious practices. For example, he taught that if we pray to God and yet "hold anything against anyone," we should forgive them so our Father in heaven can forgive us. Notice the bracing universality of Jesus's words: we should interrupt our prayers to consciously forgive *anyone for anything* (Mark 11:25).

But Jesus goes even further. He says that if you're in a religious gathering worshiping God and you "remember that your brother or sister has something against you," you should actually leave, go find them, and "be reconciled to them." It's only *after* seeking forgiveness that returning to worship has any value. Without forgiveness, church is just corrupt religiosity (Matthew 5:23-24).

Still, Jesus doesn't see forgiveness as a dry moral duty. He sees it as an infinitely creative power of new beginning that can genuinely set us free to flourish. It overcomes our most massive failures and cancels our mountain-like debts.

To illustrate this, Jesus tells a fierce story about what "the kingdom of heaven is like."

A servant owed a ridiculous debt to his king—almost $7 billion in today's currency. But the servant had nothing to his name, and so he and his family were slated to be sold as slaves.

But at the last moment, he falls on his face like Jacob, begs for mercy, and promises to repay his debt. Shockingly, the king doesn't simply agree to his impossible repayment plan. Like Esau, he completely cancels the debt and lets the man go free without paying a penny (Matthew 18:23-27).

The forgiven man now has a new start beyond his wildest dreams. But he doesn't want to truly start over.

So he hunts down a former colleague who owed him about $7,000 or one millionth of his own recently canceled debt. He puts his debtor in a chokehold and angrily demands repayment. Like himself, the man begs for patience and promises to repay. But the forgiven man refuses to give him even an extension on his debt. He has his colleague arrested and thrown into prison (Matthew 18:28-31).

When the king catches wind of this, he calls the man he forgave and interrogates him: "Shouldn't you have had mercy on your fellow servant just as I had on you?" Then he has the man thrown into prison until he can repay his $7 billion debt. Jesus concludes, "This is how my heavenly Father will treat each of you unless you forgive your brother or sister from your heart" (Matthew 18:32-35).

The point of Jesus's story isn't God's just judgment but God's extreme generosity. If our holy God is happy to freely forgive our $7 billion debt, how much more should we forgiven sinners forgive the $7,000 debts of other sinners?

Our choice to forgive reveals whether we've truly started over in God's generosity or remain imprisoned in the punitive mindset of scarcity.

Praying for Radical Depolarization

Radical depolarization is the payoff of Jesus's prayer of forgiveness.

When we honestly face our own failures, confess them, and courageously forgive others for theirs, we unmake ourselves as enemies and remake our moral solidarity. Estranged people learn to see one another as broken sisters and brothers again in God's new we. We rediscover that every human shares these core attributes in common: the dignity of divine belovedness, the reality of moral failure, and the offer of a new beginning—even for "others" as lost as Jesus's killers.

The radicalism of Jesus's depolarizing prayer becomes crystal clear when we compare it to another daily petition ironically named the "Blessing on the Heretics." This prayer became an official part of the religious liturgy around the time of Jesus. It piously pleads to God,

> "May no hope be left to the heretics… may all Your enemies be soon cut off… Blessed be You, O Lord, who strikes down enemies."[21]

This prayer expresses what many of us feel when we're honest. But notice what it does. It asks God to make others hopeless. It others people outside our group as "heretics" and "enemies." And it blends "blessing" with revenge and violence.

So Jesus—a survivor of mass violence and a victim of extremism— boldly invites us into an alternative spiritual practice. *When you think of your enemies, practice forgiving them. When you're cursed, don't curse back or fantasize about their punishment. Release their failure and bless them with a new beginning. Prioritize forgiving others even above prayer and worship.*[22]

Nelson Mandela is one of history's fiercest embodiments of this radical forgiveness.

Mandela was arrested in front of his children and spent ten thousand days of his life unjustly imprisoned under South Africa's violent apartheid system. In his autobiography *Long Walk to Freedom*, Mandela describes being dehumanized and treated like an animal in prison. He calls these seemingly endless years "unredeemably grim."

But Mandela was a follower of Jesus and writes, "I resolved not to become my own jailer." When he was released from prison, Mandela was truly free—in the world but also within his own soul. He meditates,

> "I wanted South Africa to see that I loved even my enemies
> while I hated the system that turned us against one another...
> I saw my mission as one of preaching reconciliation, of
> binding the wounds of the country, of engendering trust
> and confidence."[23]

Mandela went on to be elected as the first Black president of South Africa. And instead of unleashing retribution, Mandela created the Truth and Reconciliation Commission with Desmond Tutu to foster forgiveness in their beloved "Rainbow Nation."

For this courageous choice, President Mandela and former President de Klerk jointly won the Nobel Peace Prize. The freedom fighter Mandela chose to continue his struggle by forgiving his oppressors and seeking reconciliation even after centuries of apartheid and ten thousand days of dehumanizing imprisonment.

Mandela ruggedly reminds us that God wants to forgive us—*but never alone*. Authentic forgiveness is always shared. It depolarizes our perceptions of one another, unmakes us as enemies, and offers a new start that's stronger than prison, revenge, and death itself.

Forgiveness unlocks our future and unhostages us to radically flourish. We'll see this with fresh lucidity as we continue.

Praying with Collective Responsibility

But before we get there, notice that Jesus teaches us to pray, "Forgive *us* for *our* sins." Just like we pray to *our* Father and ask for *our* daily bread, Jesus pries open our private morality and teaches us to pray for the forgiveness of *our* sins.

With this prayer, then, Jesus subtly undermines a purely individualistic understanding of morality and awakens our collective responsibility. Recall that "I" and "me" don't appear in Jesus's prayer; it's all plural. Here Jesus challenges us to examine our participation in groups and larger systems of belonging that fail and also need God's forgiveness.

When we stop and think honestly, there are truly troubling recognitions to face.

In his book *The Power of Women*, Dr. Denis Mukwege tells the moving story of his work with women amidst war in the Democratic Republic of Congo. Congo's cyclical wars erupted in 1996, and over five million people have been killed. Congo's civil war has become the deadliest conflict since World War II.

In response, Dr. Mukwege trained to become a gynecologist and founded the Panzi Hospital in 1999 to serve survivors of the horrific sexual violence that plagues Congo still today. Dr. Mukwege's first patient had been shot in her genitals. Then an 18-month-old baby girl was rushed to his clinic as she bled profusely after being raped. To date, Dr. Mukwege's hospital has served around 70,000 rape survivors. His courageous work was recognized with the Nobel Peace Prize in 2018.

In a community meeting with survivors, an elderly widow told Dr. Mukwege the story of how she had been gang-raped by young boys in her village. After listening with a broken heart, Dr. Mukwege asked her what she needed to heal. This courageous survivor defiantly answered,

"I don't need anything. But I want one thing... I want [the President of Congo] to come and recognize our suffering and the crimes against us. That would help me heal, that would make me feel respected again by people here."[24]

This powerful woman understood collective responsibility, and she named the healing power of public confession. Like Mandela, she didn't want revenge. But she did want her society's leadership to acknowledge and apologize for the systemic evil that they had failed to prevent and that devastated her life.

In the "Preparation" to this book, we read Amanda Gorman's bracing line, "We prayed for a miracle. / What we got was a mirror."[25] The previous movements in Jesus's prayer can serve as a mirror for this self-reflective examination of our collective responsibility:

Do we still pray to a tribal "God" that privileges "us" and condemns "others"?

Do we fashion our identity and give our loyalty to a nationalistic kingdom that elevates some, lowers others, and secures itself through violent conquest?

How much of our consumeristic "more" is built on the backs of "the least of these" who labor for far less than their daily bread?

These questions interrogate our religion, politics, and economy. As individuals, we may reverently hallow God as our Father, welcome God's kingdom, and share some of our bread. But as members of an *us*, we may enjoy privileges that humiliate, oppress, and exploit others.

Many of "our" systems are laced with the addictive poison of injustice. Much of our food, phones, clothes, cars, and other commodities are stained with the invisible blood of our Father's children. Many of these sacred siblings labor within hellish mines in the Congo for the minerals that power our technology.[26] In his Nobel Prize Lecture, Dr. Mukwege stated, "Turning a blind eye to this tragedy is being complicit. It's not just perpetrators of violence who are responsible for their crimes; it is also those who choose to look the other way."[27]

Jesus's prayer, then, asks us probing questions that refuse to look away. Are we willing to pray with Jesus, "Forgive *us* for *our* sins?" Are we willing to allow prayer to become a mirror in which to examine our complicity in more-than-personal, structural, and systemic evil? What *us* do *I* inhabit that needs forgiveness and liberation from *our* sins—even if I don't see myself as personally involved in its injustice?

We discover that praying with Jesus expands the scope of our conscience for a collective responsibility. It excavates the destruction layers of our denial and frees us from false innocence. It invites us to enlarge our moral consciousness and community for a fiercer flourishing that doesn't addictively depend on exploiting others.

Unlocking the Impossible

However enlarged our moral consciousness may be, the pain of conflict is raw and can feel impossible to overcome. In *The Body Keeps the Score*, Bessel van der Kolk writes,

> "Long after a traumatic experience is over, it may be reactivated at the slightest hint of danger and mobilize disturbed brain circuits and secrete massive amounts of stress hormones. This precipitates unpleasant emotions, intense physical sensations, and impulsive and aggressive actions."[28]

We find that our loss, grief, and trauma easily lock us in the prison of the past. We fear that "if [we] start crying, [we] are never going to be able to stop."[29] The thought of releasing the "others" who have harmed us and reopening a new future in God's reconciling we, may feel revolting and intolerable.

In chapter two, we saw how Adolf Hitler exploited Germany's crushing shame, resentment, and insecurity after World War I. David Livingstone Smith observes, "Dehumanizing propaganda trades mostly on desperation, fear, and the longing for salvation."[30] This is exactly what Hitler weaponized to mobilize his genocidal Nazi movement.

In 1939, Hitler launched World War II with his invasion of Poland. By the time the war smashed to its bloody end, around six million Poles had been killed—nearly one out of every five people in the entire Polish population. Everyone knew someone who had been murdered. The Nazis' hellish extermination camps in Poland inflicted unspeakable horror, death, and trauma.[31]

A decade later, now during the Cold War, Hildegard Goss-Mayr secretly met with a group of twenty Polish Christian intellectuals. Her purpose was to ask them if they would be willing to meet with German Christians who wanted "to ask forgiveness for what Germany did to Poland during the war and to begin to build a new relationship." These Germans also understood collective responsibility.

But a member of the group answered for all with understandable outrage. He exclaimed, "What you are asking is impossible! Each stone of Warsaw has been soaked in Polish blood. We cannot forgive!"

Hildegard and her husband Jean pleaded with their Polish friends to reconsider. How could healing begin unless followers of Jesus would take the first courageous step? But they were entrenched and concluded, "This is not yet the time for forgiveness."

Hildegard recounts the unexpected outcome of their meeting in prayer:

"Even after a decade, the war wounds remained fresh and deep. Jean and I saw we could go no further. It was getting late. Before separating, we proposed that we recite together the prayer that unites us all, the Our Father.

All joined willingly. But when we got to the passage, 'and forgive us our sins as we forgive...,' our Polish friends halted in the prayer.

Into this silence, the one who had said, 'It is impossible' spoke in a low voice: 'I must say yes to you. I could no more pray the Our Father, I could no longer call myself a Christian, if I refuse to forgive. Humanly speaking, I cannot do it, but God will give us the strength!'"

This is what praying with Jesus can unlock. We enter into a halting silence in which the pain-filled words *It is impossible!* break open into a new confession of hope: *God will give us the strength!* A new beginning is born.

Ten of these Polish survivors went on to participate in the first East-West International Fellowship of Reconciliation conference with their German neighbors. Hildegard recalls, "From this meeting, many initiatives in East-West relations began. The friendships and consequences continue until today."[32]

It's important to note that these Polish survivors didn't deny the horrors they had suffered or pretend like the evil of the past wasn't real. Forgiveness is not forgetfulness. In fact, they named that *every stone* of their city was soaked with blood. Moral amnesia is dangerous on the human level and not what Jesus asks of us.

But as these survivors practiced with Jesus, they creatively rebelled against the hatred and violence that had driven the genocide they survived. With courage and compassion, they chose a divine power more radical than the hideous evil of Hitler's death camps.

And like Mandela, their forgiveness unlocked the prison of the past and unhostaged them for the healing of a previously unimaginable we. Europe embarked on a new beginning of peace that has endured for over seventy-five years. Today this peace is being severely tested once again.

Begin Again

Forgiveness is this original and ultimate freedom from evil's totalitarian prison. Rather than reacting, it acts. Rather than copying, it creates. Rather than holding on to pain, it holds on to people. When everything appears to be over and new beginnings impossible, forgiveness starts rewriting our story and unlocks a new future of hope. Its flower breaks through the stony mountainside of our failure, and the pain of our past begins to erode with courageous healing and magnificent beauty.

This freedom is what Jesus invites us to embrace in the second half of his passionate prayer. It's spiritual practice for a mature flourishing that emancipates us from our deadly denial.

First, Jesus calls us to look in the mirror and honestly confess our failures to God. Rather than rejection, what we find is that our Father still accepts us and wants to forgive us. Our divine connection is safe and secure. We are beloved, and we can be set free to begin again. With time and reimmersion in the waters of our divine belovedness, our shame is washed away, and we slowly learn to forgive ourselves.

Second, Jesus challenges us that we cannot be forgiven alone. Authentic forgiveness is always shared and reforges the we of God's sacred family, including our enemies. Without this, our personal forgiveness remains a false start. Mandela is one of the most inspiring examples in history of this shared freedom.

Finally, Jesus expands the scope of our responsibility for a fierce flourishing that depolarizes people and doesn't depend on dehumanizing anyone. Dr. Mukwege and the rape survivors of Congo powerfully remind us of our collective responsibility.

Facing past and future, forgiveness is how we begin again, even after devastating loss and genocidal trauma. It's how Polish survivors processed their pain and chose reconciliation with their repentant German neighbors. It's why Karin Sokel, whom we met in chapter one, was able to envision even holding on to Adolf Hitler when heaven comes to earth.[33]

Jesus defiantly proclaimed forgiveness to the very end of his earthly life. We witness that Jesus actually *meant* it when he prayed, "Father, forgive them, for they don't know what they're doing." After outliving his own brutal murder, Jesus didn't hold on to his pain and unleash revengeful retribution. Jesus released his pain and invited his followers to launch a global movement of forgiveness for *everyone*.

This is how Jesus commissioned his practitioners as they prepared to embark on this movement:

> "Peace be with you! Just like the Father sent me, I'm now sending you. If you forgive anyone's sins, their sins are forgiven."[34] (John 20:21-23)

The matter-of-factness of Jesus's promise is powerful. If you forgive anyone's sins, their sins are forgiven. It's finished. New beginning.

This was Jesus's original and enduring mission. As we pray with Jesus today, each one of us can become a hotspot of forgiveness streaming a global network of new beginnings for *anyone*. Evil is unoriginal and not the end of our story. Our divine beginning is real and resilient. Mental health, relational healing, and public reconciliation are its promises for us today.

But as Jesus's own biography painfully illustrates, practicing this kind of prayerful life is disruptive to the status quo and won't go unopposed. And stopping with forgiveness may not dig deep enough into the hidden roots of why we have conflict to begin with and fail to prevent the painful cycle of conflict from escalating.

It's to this reality of risk and the premeditation of nonviolence that Jesus takes us next.

There is more to practice.

Practice Flourishing

Dig through denial, search yourself, and make a list of the individuals and/or the groups that you're tempted to see as unrelated or less than you. If you quickly jump to the conclusion that you don't have anyone like this in your life, you're not alone. But most of us do when we honestly look in the mirror of Jesus's prayer. Usually our bodies tell the truth: whose face do you not want to see, whose voice do you not want to hear, whose presence do you not want to share? Make a list.

Then commit to praying for these people every day for the next week. Try using this sample prayer and/or writing your own:

Our Father,

I'm not sure that I want to forgive these people. I confess that it's easier to avoid or attack them. It's uncomfortable and painful to even pray for them. My emotions are difficult to face and manage. I feel ashamed and angry.

But you have given me this choice, and I choose to forgive the people who have hurt me. Please heal what is hurting, broken, and causing conflict in them. Please heal what is hurting, broken, and causing conflict in me. Liberate us from resentment and empower us to desire one another's flourishing.

We are we, and we open ourselves to receive and share your gift of a new beginning.

Amen.

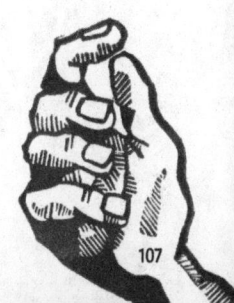

Chapter 6

Can Violence Save Us?
Deliver Us from Evil

A Practice of Premeditated Nonviolence

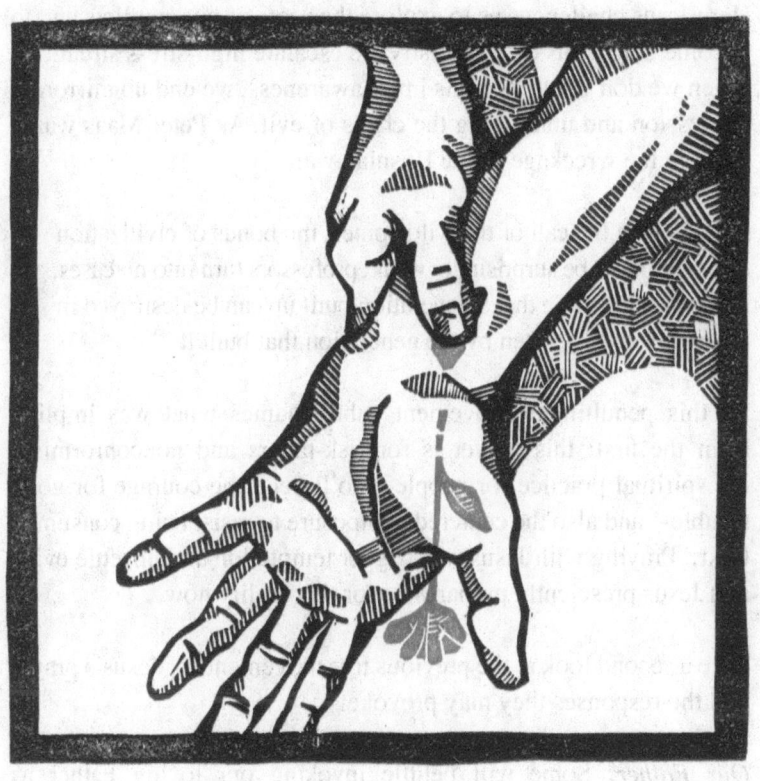

"Face your fears / Look for salvation when troubles get real."
Kendrick Lamar[1]

"Training is as necessary for [nonviolence] as for armed revolt...
The badge of the violent is his weapon—spear, or sword, or rifle.
God is the shield of the nonviolent."
Mohandas Gandhi[2]

Praying for Good Trouble

Jesus has just invited us to practice the courageous healing of forgiveness. He now takes us a step deeper into our spiritual adulthood, from resolving our conflicts into transforming them before they begin.

Here Jesus challenges us to explore the roots of our conflicts and to become conscious of how easily we escalate high-stress situations. When we don't cultivate this inner awareness, we end up mirroring aggression and unleashing the chaos of evil. As Peter Maas warns us from the wreckage of the Bosnian war,

> "[W]hen the call of the wild comes, the bonds of civilization turn out to be surprisingly weak, professors turn into nutcases, and everything that a generation built up can be destroyed in a day or two, often by the generation that built it."[3]

So this penultimate movement subtly names what was implicit from the first: this prayer is for risk-takers and nonconformists. It's spiritual practice for people who'll need the courage for good trouble—and also the centered composure to resist being consumed by it.[4] Praying with Jesus will trigger temptation and unsettle evil— and Jesus presciently prepares us for this reality now.

Take a second look at the previous five movements of Jesus's prayer and the responses they may provoke:

Our Father: Some will belittle invoking our loving Father as sentimental nonsense and a threat to their closed, human-controlled worldview. They'll dismiss it as too "religious" or "conservative." Others will condemn practicing our divine belovedness as subversive to their exclusive religion and a threat to their dualistic, hierarchical worldview. They'll dismiss it as "heretical" or "liberal." Ironically, supposedly secular and religious camps alike may find common cause in discrediting this God and attacking the children who call God our Parent. Recall that priests and politicians teamed up to execute Jesus.

Hallowed Be Your Name: Some will resist reverencing G-d and refuse to surrender their religious certainty. Since ancient times, humans have grasped for G-d's name as a weapon for power. We habitually try to pocket "God" as trump for our tribe, a mascot for our ambitions, or a coping mechanism for our private problems. So humble hallowers may be denounced as doubters and deconstructors, as mystics and enemies to any unhallowed handling of God. Real reverence will be ridiculed as wishy-washy relativism or a rebellious suspicion of the religious "fathers."

Your Kingdom Come: Some will see welcoming and working for God's kingdom as disloyal and dangerous to their own. People who prayerfully participate in our Father's dream may be targeted as troublemakers who disrupt the status quo or as traitors who refuse to pledge loyalty to whichever group or nation is being sold as exceptional or under siege. Some will insult them as "utopians" or "social justice warriors." Like Jesus, they may experience the irony of enemies becoming opportunistic friends to oppose them.

Give Us Our Daily Bread: Some will write-off the kingdom's economy of our daily bread as both too little and too much—as anything but enough. The successful and respectable may see Jesus's followers' subversive simplicity as too minimalist and meager. Others will see their emphasis on our shared needs and resources as "socialist" and threatening to private affluence. This practice's conscious retraining of our appetite will confuse and aggravate the champions of individualistic surplus, security, and status as the marks of real success.

Forgive Us as We Forgive Others: People who make forgiveness their daily practice may be the most threatening of all. Their courageous honesty surrenders denial and faces troubling recognitions—both present and past. Their desire for healing unlocks the profitable prison system of shame, blame, and hate by holding on to people and releasing pain. Their commitment to new beginnings drains the gas tank of polarization, dehumanization, and retribution. Some will denounce them as "secularists" or "heretics" for prioritizing forgiveness over private piety and religious performances. Others will label them "terrorists" for wanting reconciliation with "the enemy."

In short, our spiritual practice with Jesus will not go uncontested. It may even be angrily condemned and violently opposed. Jesus's own biography with its death threats, bogus arrest, and brutal execution is a sobering illustration of this.

Spiritual practice with Jesus, then, will trigger what he calls "temptation." These are high-stress, fight-or-flight situations that easily unleash the chaos of evil within us and between us. These destabilizing trials tell us that we can only be truly safe if we harden ourselves and meet aggression on its own terms. They block the creativity of forgiveness and end up mimicking what they claim to overcome. They whisper or scream that only violence can truly save us.[5]

The outcomes can be disastrous as we saw in Germany and Bosnia. We look back in the wreckage of these dizzying turning points and realize how profoundly they devastate our lives and histories. We ask with disbelief and heartbreak, *How did that even happen? Why did it go so far and spin so badly out of control? What were we thinking?*

From the smoldering ashes, we see afresh why forgiveness is so urgently important—and how it quickly becomes so seemingly impossible.

So we face this sobering question before conflict even begins: Can violence actually save us when everything is on the line? Or is there a better way that can take us through temptation and deliver us from evil for a new beginning of healing and hope?

Our Good Friday Temptation

Not long after Lily and I got Eyob's prophetic video message, sold our stuff, and moved back to Ethiopia, praying with Jesus led us into another risky transition.

Massive protests erupted in Ethiopia against decades of violent political oppression. The government cracked down brutally by imposing a nationwide state of emergency and imprisoning tens of thousands of people. Many were killed. Predictably, this violent response only escalated the crisis further.

Horrifying images began to appear in social media uncovering the mass violence that was being unleashed. A gruesome picture went viral of a man being lynched naked and upside down from a traffic sign as hundreds of people watched him die. Then a video emerged of a young school teacher pouring gasoline on the bodies of two men who had been beaten and left dazed not far from where Eyob grew up. She lit a match, set them on fire, raised her hands in triumph, and watched them burn alive. It was hideous and traumatizing to watch.

Both public executions happened in city centers not too far from Addis. As the violence escalated, the United Nations reported that Ethiopia had the highest number of internally displaced people in the world—more than war-torn countries like Syria and Congo.

I remember sitting in my office at the Ethiopian Graduate School of Theology and talking to the pictures on my bookshelf. Eyob, Dietrich Bonhoeffer, Martin Luther King, and Oscar Romero stared back at me. With bewildered grief, I asked them, *What is the meaning of responsibility? What is Jesus asking us to do in this time of temptation?*

Soon enough, it became clear to me that I couldn't stay put on the safe island of Christian academia detached from a society in crisis. The school's president had already warned me twice to stop speaking openly against injustice. I was a professor of *public* theology, but the acceptable theology was purely *private*.

So I submitted my resignation letter. Lily, I, and our partner Dr. Tekalign Nega then launched the Neighbor-Love Movement. Our mission was to inspire young Ethiopians to see and treat others as precious neighbors rather than strangers or enemies in this explosive time of escalating conflict.

We started knocking on every door we could and traveling the country. We spoke to large audiences of youth on university campuses and created a social media campaign that has reached over twenty million people. We invited our audiences to sign our Neighbor-Love Covenant, to embody its seven practices, and to become ambassadors of love and justice across our diverse identities for a peaceful Ethiopia where people could flourish.

Thousands of youth signed our covenant. And we were encouraged as our work quickly won small grants from the U.S. Embassy in Ethiopia, the Bank of America, and the European Institute of Peace.[6]

But peace is threatening to those who profit from conflict.

Like many places in our world, Ethiopia's public life is dominated by powerful group identities that mobilize around (in)famous leaders. I call them "(in)famous" because some see these leaders as God-sent messiahs promising salvation. But others see them as demonic monsters who threaten to create hell on earth.

This extreme polarization supercharges othering as David Livingstone Smith observed: "Dehumanizing propaganda trades mostly on desperation, fear, and the longing for salvation." And Smith was sadly right about the grim outcomes: "given the right circumstances, virtually all of us are capable of slipping into the dehumanizing mindset, and committing acts of cruelty that would otherwise be difficult or even impossible for us to perform."[7]

This is exactly what we saw erupting in Ethiopia as we built the Neighbor-Love Movement. Othering and enraged revenge were unleashing public executions, horrifying massacres, ethnic cleansing, and weaponized rape. Prime Minister Abiy won the Nobel Peace Prize in 2019 but carelessly escalated the conflict into civil war in November 2020.

As I write, Ethiopia remains locked in this grievous civil war. The conflict has killed as many as 500,000 people, created famine for almost a million others, and displaced millions more from their homes.[8] Today Ethiopia's genocide alert level is at 9 out of 10—the stage designated "Elimination" just before the final stage of "Denial."[9]

In the early days of the Neighbor-Love Movement, my friend Dr. Solomon at the African Union challenged me to go to "the unconverted" and build relationship with these (in)famous leaders. I accepted Solomon's challenge with a curious gulp of fear and hope.

I started in jail with Eskinder Nega, an (in)famous leader imprisoned on charges of inciting violence. From jail, I went all the way to the soon-to-be Attorney General of Ethiopia, Dr. Gedion Timothewos. My goal was to pray with these leaders, to earn their trust, and to encourage them to promote neighbor-love and nonviolent dialogue. My thesis was simple but challenging: If these iconic, group-mobilizing leaders could meet with one another and model dialogue, perhaps civil war could be averted and ordinary Ethiopians could flourish.

I'll never forget the day that I visited Eskinder again after his release from prison, this time at his political party's headquarters. I pleaded with Eskinder to take the courageous step of meeting to dialogue with Jawar Mohammed, one of his arch-rivals with over two million followers on Facebook. But after praying together and an initial promise to do this, Eskinder was unwilling and told me that Ethiopia needed its own "war on terror."[10]

After praying with Eskinder, I got in a taxi and crossed Addis to visit the home of none other than Jawar Mohammed. Jawar had invited me to break the Ramadan fast with him on his birthday, and I brought him my partner Tekalign's new book *Balinjeraye*, or *Neighbor-Love*, as a gift. It was a wonderful night of conversation with wildly diverse people. Jawar was willing to dialogue, but it takes two to tango.[11]

These men were seen by millions of Ethiopians as irreconcilable enemies, as messiahs or monsters who would lead Ethiopia to salvation or civil war. But my mission with both was the same: to pray together, to build relationship, and to encourage dialogue and reconciliation. Getting in the same room together would have been a significant breakthrough as the conflict continued escalating.

It nearly worked. I'd scoped out a secure hotel room where we were set to record their conversation. But, alas, Eskinder refused at the last minute, and it never happened. Shortly after, both men were imprisoned on charges of inciting violence.[12]

Lily's and my temptation began ironically on Good Friday 2020. I started receiving dozens of death threats. Before long, I had gotten over sixty murderous messages accompanied by terrifying images of men holding machine guns. A 20-minute "documentary" was made about me by militant figures with hundreds of thousands of followers on Facebook. They claimed that I had a "hidden agenda" to destroy Ethiopia and that this was my sinister reason for crossing enemy lines. Their YouTube video quickly racked up over 50,000 views and instigated more terroristic threats.

People sent me messages about how they would butcher my body, throw me off a bridge, and run me over with their cars. Lily and I lived near a busy road with numerous butcher shops and a big bridge, so these threats hit very close to home. But what cut me closest to the heart was something else: most of these violent messages came from people who publicly identified as devout *Christians*. One man wrote that his "allegiance to the cross" gave him a *duty* to kill me. In his violent kingdom, meeting with "the enemy" was intolerable treason.

I quickly learned a painful but powerful lesson. Many of us see the practices in Jesus's prayer as deeply threatening and worthy of suspicion—if not ferocious, terroristic opposition. We might be able to recite Jesus's prayer in our sleep and mouth it at church with our tribe. But actually *practicing* Jesus's spirituality depolarizes our identities and unlocks our militant loyalties. Transgressing these entrenched cultural boundaries easily triggers explosive anger and violent aggression. When you love the enemy, you become the enemy.

These trials are severe. They test whether we'll conform to aggression, run away, or press deeper into our *practice*—that difficult choice to flourish even when we don't feel it. The intensity of this mortal danger does strange things to us. Adrenaline surges. Sleep vanishes. The mind spins. The heart races. Fear and anger erupt within us. Distress burns in our bodies and tries to conform us.

And so we face one of conflict's most perverse ironies: we feel magnetically pulled to imitate the behavior that threatens to destroy us. Something deep inside our bones and brains tells us to react to insults with insults, intimidation with intimidation, aggression with aggression. The result can only be escalation.[13]

Lily and I discovered the obvious but often ignored reality: without *premeditated* practice of nonviolence, these situations catch us by surprise. Soon enough, they spin out of control and escalate into evil's catastrophic chaos. The outcome is devastation—whether this looks like broken personal relationships or a brutal civil war that unleashes suffering on millions of people.

Jesus's Mindful Presence

Jesus anticipates this temptation with prescient sobriety. He understood the risks of prayerfully practicing with him. And so Jesus teaches us a practice of *premeditated* nonviolence to prepare for these high-stress, chaotic conflicts before they even begin. He invites us to pray, *Don't lead us into temptation but deliver us from evil* (Matthew 6:12; Luke 11:4).[14]

This penultimate movement of prayer is the opposite of a macho chant for heroes with messiah complexes. It silences the battle cry that boasts, "Bring it on!" This prayer simultaneously resists suppressing our distress and escalating our conflict.

In the face of violence, then, Jesus teaches us to become conscious of our vulnerability and to confess our hope. We are temptable, fragile people, and we will experience temptation-triggering crises.

But the evil of conflict is not our destination. When we anchor ourselves in prayerful nonviolence, God promises to lead us *through* these distressing situations into deliverance. Professor Howard Thurman, the mentor of Martin Luther King Jr., wrote,

> "To be assured of this becomes the answer to the threat of violence—yes, to violence itself. To the degree to which a person knows *this*, he is unconquerable from within and without."[15]

This is what we witness in Jesus's final hours as the distress of temptation and the mindfulness of prayer collide.

Hate speech, death threats, and violent plots ignite against Jesus. Crushing pressure rapidly builds in his biography. Each scene shutters with another perspective on what's coming:

Scene 1: Jesus warns his students that he's about to be murdered (Matthew 26:1-2).

Scene 2: The religious and cultural leaders plot to arrest and execute Jesus (Matthew 26:3-5).

Scene 3: A woman at a leper's house pours perfume on Jesus's body, and he embraces this as preparation for his burial (Matthew 26:6-13).

Scene 4: Judas gets paid off and agrees to orchestrate Jesus's arrest (Matthew 26:14-16).

Scene 5: Jesus shares a last supper with his disciples and discusses the violence that's coming. He describes his suffering body as a gift of forgiveness and healing that will clinch the coming of God's kingdom (Matthew 26:17-30; Luke 22:15).

Scene 6: At last, Jesus takes his followers to a mountainside overlooking Jerusalem. He warns them once more that he's about to be killed and that they'll run away before the night is finished (Matthew 26:31-35).

Notice Jesus's mindful presence throughout these scenes.

First, Jesus directly names the violent temptation that's about to erupt. He verbally processes the distress of dying with honesty and vulnerability in the presence of his closest friends.

Second, Jesus feeds his body and decides in advance that he won't run away or fight against this suffering. He will accept it and pass through, anchored in his own creative freedom. Thich Nhat Hanh called Jesus's last supper "a mindfulness meal."[16]

Third, Jesus confesses his hope: healing will overcome this terrible evil because divine forgiveness is stronger than human violence. What presents itself as the end is just the beginning. The kingdom of heaven is coming, come what may.

We watch as Jesus *premeditates* nonviolent sobriety against addictive distress. He anticipates the overwhelming temptation that's about to explode. In this way, he actively resists distracting himself or denying this painful reality. He prepares himself to pass *through* temptation by trusting in God as his deliverer—not by imitating and escalating his attackers.

Satanic Temptation

But Jesus's closest follower Peter is in a totally different state of mind.

Peter interrupts Jesus and declares that he's ready to fight to the death for Jesus and his kingdom. For Peter and for many of us today, violence is the addictive shortcut out of our distress and the ultimate expression of our loyalty.[17]

Peter's outburst echoes back to a heated argument between him and Jesus soon before. There Peter had confessed that Jesus was "the Messiah, the Son of the living God." Jesus affirmed Peter's faith and called it the cornerstone of the kingdom. But Jesus told him to keep it secret and added something totally unexpected and seemingly anti-messianic. He explained that he was about to "suffer many things and be killed." This is how God's kingdom would ultimately come (Matthew 16:16-21).

Peter was outraged and passionately rebuked Jesus for his sacrificial vision of saving the world. He exclaimed with certainty, "This will never happen to you!" (Matthew 16:22).

We see that Peter was still a religious nationalist.[18] He found it revolting that the Messiah would suffer and die. Peter believed that the real Messiah would deliver Israel by defeating his nation's enemies—not by suffering for their shared salvation. For Peter, nonviolent sacrifice was *failure*—not the fulfillment of our *flourishing*.

Jesus responds to Peter with his harshest rebuke on record. The intensity of Jesus's tone and the severity of his words indicate their urgent importance. He tells Peter,

> "Get behind me, Satan! You are a trigger trap to me, because you don't have in mind what concerns God but merely what concerns people. Whoever wants to practice with me must say no to their very selves, get ready for execution, and follow me.
>
> Here's the deal: anybody who wants to save their life is going to lose it; but anybody who loses their life because of me will find their life. What's the point of someone gaining the whole world but giving up their life in the process?" (Matthew 16:23-26; see Luke 4:13; 8:12-14)

For Jesus, the idea that violence can save us from suffering is the very personification of Satan—the original liar and tempter. It's the alluring but empty illusion of empire: *Monopolize power, dominate others, and then you'll be truly safe*.

Howard Thurman understood this seductive mindset. He wrote,

> "*How not to be killed* becomes the great end, and morality takes its meaning from that center. Until that center is shifted, nothing real can be accomplished."[19]

Like Jesus insisted, the imperial way ends up splintering the soul. It makes us all losers and only cuts us off from the flourishing we desire. It's a suicide mission sold as salvation.

Jesus trusted God to secure a fiercer flourishing for us. It passes *through* suffering—and then out beyond its grasp. This is why Jesus queered Rome's cross into the rugged symbol of his movement. The paradox of the kingdom is that we can seemingly lose everything and yet still be perfectly safe in God's unseen hands.

Only this premeditated trust can lead to real salvation, even if it looks like loss in the short run. Jesus calls us to rethink what the world means through the crucible of suffering. This is the true test of *metanoia*—the revolution in the mind that opens us into the kingdom of heaven.

But Peter was entrenched, and his violent mindset remained unchanged. With suffering threatening to explode, he insisted that he was ready to kill and be killed for Jesus. In fact, all of Jesus's followers imitate Peter and confess the same.

We need to pause in this moment of astonishing honesty in Jesus's biography.

These young men were his closest students. He handpicked them, and they were with him daily for three years as he traveled, taught, and healed. They were there when he first introduced his prayer to the crowd outside Nazareth.

And yet the satanic mindset of violent salvation remained stronger in them than Jesus's own spiritual practice. Jesus's students flunked their final test. Even for them, Jesus's vision of God and human flourishing through suffering remained too foreign and fierce to truly trust.

Jesus's Premeditated Nonviolence

But Jesus wasn't derailed into another argument. His response is striking and can serve as a paradigm of nonviolence for us to follow today as we prepare for our own temptations.

First, Jesus takes his followers for a walk to a garden. He gets their bodies moving, their lungs breathing, and relocates them to a place of calm beauty.

Neurochemical research on high-conflict situations indicates how important physical movement is for resetting our thinking and creating the openness for composure in crisis. Jesus had befriended his body and apparently understood this.[20]

Second, Jesus models the heart of all real practice: he honestly faces the distress building within himself and confesses his grief.

Of course, the alternative was easier. Jesus could have denied or bottled up his explosive emotion. But Jesus does the opposite. He names it, sets it in the light, and shares it with his friends. We hear Jesus tell them, "My soul is overwhelmed with grief to the point of death" (Matthew 26:38).

Elizabeth Kübler-Ross writes,

> "Telling the story helps to dissipate the pain. Telling your story often and in detail is primal to the grieving process. You must get it out. Grief must be witnessed to be healed. Grief shared is grief abated."[21]

This is exactly what Jesus does with his grief. And so Jesus takes control of his feelings, regulates his nervous system, and invites his friends to become aware of their own surging emotions. As the psychologist Carl Rogers wrote, "Once an experience is fully in awareness, fully accepted, then it can be coped with effectively, like any other clear reality."[22]

Third, Jesus calls his students to center themselves in prayer—to soak their conscious attention in God's presence.

Unsurprisingly, this prayer wasn't spontaneous. It was an intensified practice of his penultimate movement:

> "Be awake and *pray so that you will not fall into temptation.*
> The spirit is willing, but the flesh is weak." (Matthew 26:41;
> Mark 13:38; Luke 22:40)

Here at the end, pulsing with anguish, Jesus takes his students back to the beginning—back to the bedrock of his spirituality. Being prayerfully present with our Father is the only deliverance through the hijacking illusion that we can save ourselves with violence. With God, we are still safe, even in our gravest danger.

As the world spins and flashes before our eyes, we can listen once more for the Voice of our divine belovedness: *You are my beloved children; I delight in you. You can still trust me.*[23]

Peter's Blackout

But Jesus's premeditated nonviolence is, simply put, *difficult*. It's certainly not our instinctive response to violent temptation. As Gandhi understood, "Training is as necessary for [nonviolence] as for armed revolt."[24] Howard Thurman called this "a discipline, a method, a technique, as over against some form of wishful thinking or simple desiring." It's "made possible only by personal triumph."[25]

Peter was apparently still inadequately practiced. Rather than staying awake and praying through his temptation, he checks out and falls asleep. He deals with his distress by avoiding it and blacking out.[26]

Of course, our addictions are many, and we deal with our distress in different ways. We may lose sleep, abuse substances, exploit sex, over work, binge on media, or blackout in another way. In whichever form, this de-presencing avoidance leaves us vulnerable to crumbling to our temptation, and this is exactly what happens to Peter.

An armed militia shows up in the garden, and Judas cynically identifies Jesus with a kiss. Jesus is seized, and Peter loses all control. His fight reaction takes over. Peter grabs a sword and starts swinging for people's heads. In fact, he targets Malchus, the personal assistant to the cleric who masterminded Jesus's arrest, and hacks off his ear (Matthew 26:50-51; Luke 22:49; John 18:10).

Jesus's biography braces here with even greater honesty. Peter was one of the first to answer Jesus's call to *metanoia* and quickly became Jesus's star protege. He was there when Jesus taught the crowd to pray, "Don't lead us into temptation but deliver us from evil." He even received Jesus's personal rebuke for his violent vision of salvation and woke up to hear Jesus's triple plea to prayerfully practice through his temptation.

But like so many of us, Peter was physically "there" but somewhere else in his soul. His mind was still running on Jacob's ancient operating system of grasping for power and crediting "God" with the spoils. Deep in his brain and bones—what Jesus calls our "flesh"—Peter was still convinced that violence was the way of salvation. So he was sure that he could save the Savior with his sword—not by suffering and trusting God's deliverance.

The results were ironic and pitiful, as they often are in our lives and conflicts. Peter merely succeeded in chopping off Malchus's ear. In doing so, he ironically amputated the organ that Jesus insisted embodies the kingdom's nonviolence: *listening* to the truth.

Evil's chaos is unleashed as Peter spins with temptation. The disciples run for their lives. The police abuse and insult Jesus. The religious leaders spit on him and stir up the crowd to have him crucified. Peter is so enraged by Jesus's nonviolent response that he denies even knowing him and breaks down with bitter weeping. Judas commits suicide.[27]

We know this chaos all too well still today. It's a kaleidoscopic episode raging with fear, grief, and violence.

The Most Defiantly Beautiful Death in History

But Jesus's premeditation prevails. He is centered and composed throughout the most anguishing hours of his life. We witness a person possessed of defiant freedom and healing creativity when only aggressive reactivity and powerless suffering seem possible.

When Judas steps forward to betray him, Jesus addresses Judas as *friend*. He meets his most intimate enemy with disarming dignity and resists soothing his own distress by using escalating insults (Matthew 26:50).

When Jesus's disciples draw their weapons to defeat violence with violence, Jesus cries out,

> "No more violence! Put your sword back in its place! For all
> who draw the sword will die by the sword!" (Luke 22:51;
> Matthew 26:52-56).

As Dr. King learned from Jesus, "Nonviolence is a weapon fabricated of love. It is a sword that heals."[28] Jesus remains lucid and resolute. Salvation by violence is an addictive illusion that can only kill us.

When Peter hacks off Malchus's ear, Jesus reaches out and touches him. Jesus doesn't take pleasure in Malchus's pain or declare that justice has been served. Jesus uses his power to heal his enemy and restore his capacity to listen.

And when Jesus gets interrogated by the religious leaders and punched in the face, Jesus challenges them with facts and questions. He says that his movement was always public and nonviolent, so why arrest him at night with an armed militia? He protests their violence without crumbling or copying it, saying "If I said something wrong, point it out. But if I spoke the truth, why are you abusing me?" (John 18:23).

Here we pick up where we left off in chapter three.

Jesus finally stands before the Governor of Jerusalem under the charge of "subverting the nation." Pilate interrogates Jesus for treason, and Jesus impenitently answers that he has a rival kingdom. But this kingdom operates without violence, and that's why he stopped his followers from fighting for him. The real kingdom can only be defended by truth and listening, the pillars of peaceful deliberative process. And so Jesus asks Pilate questions and engages him in dialogue (Luke 23:2; John 18:33-37).

Pilate hardens himself and asks, "Don't you realize that I have power either to free you or to crucify you?" It's as if Pilate is confused and exasperated by Jesus's defiant dignity. This young carpenter is a decision away from being tortured and executed; and yet he doesn't cower or beg for mercy. He remains unafraid and unrepentant, like an equal to his oppressor but claiming a higher power.[29]

What happens next is one of the most psychologically profound scenes in human history.

Jesus is tortured and then slowly asphyxiated on a Roman cross. Religious leaders, government officials, and rebel fighters all unite in tempting Jesus with the same slogan: "Save yourself!" Ironically, these bitter enemies aligned around a common enemy and a shared ideology: salvation comes through violence.

In fact, the crowd humiliates Jesus with cutting language from his own prayer: "Let God *deliver* him now if he *wants* him." These shaming words viciously attacked the core of Jesus's spirituality—his own divine belovedness. They insist that pain and powerlessness are irrefutable proof of being *unwanted* and *abandoned* by God (Luke 23:35-39; Matthew 27:43).

But Jesus's premeditation prevails once more. He isn't overpowered by doubt, rage, and aggression. Instead, he invokes the presence of our Father and continues his spiritual practice amidst his pain. Jesus dies the beautifully defiant death in history; he flourishes to the end.

We watch Jesus cry out with forgiveness for his killers. He prays, "Father, forgive them, for they don't know what they're doing." Jesus recognized that these people were *un*premeditated. They were off balance and out of control, dealing with their distress by mirroring the violence that oppressed them. So Jesus doesn't damn them to hell; he asks God to give them a new beginning (Luke 23:34).

Jesus then promises the kingdom to the rebel being crucified beside him. Execution was designed to isolate and end victims—to erase their future and hope. But Jesus rebels against this nihilism. He assures his fellow criminal of their safe connection with God and unbreakable hope beyond suffering in the kingdom of heaven: "Today you will be with me in paradise" (Luke 23:40-43).

Finally, Jesus lets go and confesses his grief-filled trust in God: "Father, into your hands I commit my spirit." His final breath protests against the taunt that our suffering proves we're unwanted by God. Jesus disbelieves the voice of shame and trusts in the Voice of divine belovedness that birthed his movement. Death is not the end. It's a new beginning of being held by God's hands and ushered into the kingdom of heaven (Luke 23:46; Matthew 27:46-50; Mark 15:34-37).

Sticking the Landing When Our World Is Spinning

How was it possible for Jesus to die like this—with defiant forgiveness, rebellious hope, and unbreakable trust in God?

The best analogy I've found comes from the world of gymnastics.

In 2008, Anastasia Liukin won All-Around Champion at the Olympics. In trial after trial, her task was to fling herself into the air, twirl her body in every direction, and then *stick the landing*. This meant landing fully centered on her feet without falling or even stumbling—and with her head held high.

As I watch Liukin's trials, her landings almost look unreal. Her high-speed rolling, flipping, and twirling make losing control and falling on her face seem inevitable. Staying centered and actually landing on her feet appear unbelievable and humanly impossible.

And yet, she did it—again and again. Liukin stuck her landings. And so she was awarded the world's highest gymnastic recognition.[30]

Of course, Liukin's triumph on the global stage wasn't due to luck or divine intervention. It was the climax of her unseen, daily *practice* combining control and surrender amidst dizzying distress. Liukin captures her Olympic craft in a tight paradox: "Being a gymnast is having the strength to hold on and the courage to let go."[31]

This is exactly what we witness in Jesus's nonviolent protest and beautifully defiant death.

At first sight, the forgiving, hope-sharing, trusting way that Jesus died may seem unbelievable and impossible. How did he resist fighting back or cursing his enemies or simply collapsing under the pressure of so much physical and psychological pain?

But Jesus had been practicing with premeditation for this moment. We know he did this for at least three years. And so none of these movements were new to Jesus or improvised out of thin air. In prayer, Jesus had died a thousand times before he died.

In the end, the way Jesus died was really the climax of the way Jesus lived—and the paradoxical fulfillment of his flourishing. Jesus was able to stick the landing in the final trial of his life because of his premeditated practice of prayer:

1. Talking with our loving Father and disbelieving the shame of being unwanted.

2. Reverencing G-d's holy Mystery and refusing to weaponize "God" for power.

3. Welcoming the kingdom's healing and remaining resolute in its nonviolent witness against injustice.

4. Trusting God to care for our bodily needs even when the next moment is uncertain and insecure.

5. Holding on to people and releasing the pain they cause through forgiveness.

6. Premeditating nonviolence in distress and refusing to unleash further evil in response to aggression.

This prayerful practice gave Jesus the centered strength to hold on and the rugged courage to let go. He didn't flail or fall on his face. He held his head high, forgave his killers, shared hope with a dead man, and trusted God with his own death.

In short, Jesus *practiced* flourishing—daily and unseen, for years. And so he was able to flourish to the bitter end—and then beyond it, as we'll see in our last chapter. With brilliant irony, Howard Thurman called Jesus's death "a spiritual triumph of staggering proportions."[32]

Our Deliverance

Prayerful practice with Jesus is risky business. It'll inevitably stir up good trouble within us and between us. And it will unsettle evil and confront us with our addictive habit of trusting violence to save us. In the ruins, we look back and see that violence only escalates our conflicts and unleashes more evil in a vicious cycle of imitation.

So Jesus calls us to face our temptation head-on and to premeditate nonviolence before the cycle even starts. We know that these distressing situations are coming. There's no getting around them, and they'll make us feel like the world is spinning.

But they're not our destination, and they don't need to conform or consume us. They're part of our journey *through* suffering into God's deliverance. As Amanda Gorman writes, "What endures isn't always what escapes."[33] And so we pray, "Don't lead us into temptation but deliver us from evil."

This was Jesus's own practice, and his premeditated nonviolence prevailed to the end. Still today, it can prepare us to flourish even when flourishing seems impossible.

With Jesus we learn to breathe, befriend our bodies, and center our consciousness in God's deliverance. We face our temptability with full presence and verbally process our distressing grief with others. We speak with dignity, share hope, and disbelieve shame's insistence that God doesn't want us. As New Testament scholar N.T. Wright observes, "By giving us this prayer, then, Jesus invites us to walk ahead into the darkness and discover that it, too, belongs to God."[34]

This penultimate prayer takes us into a divine darkness. It fuels a fiercer flourishing that was foreign to Peter and that remains unfamiliar to popular spirituality still today. In it, we discover that the peak of our flourishing may not look like health, wealth, and winning. It looks like being able to face our deepest fears, to talk about them openly with our friends, to share the pain of other victims, and to trust God to deliver us. In doing so, we transform our pain rather than transmitting it.[35]

To stick *this* landing is radically fierce flourishing. It's how the cycle of violence stops and how we get to the roots of our conflicts. It's how we not only forgive one another but go deep enough into ourselves to prevent evil from being unleashed in the first place.

Peace advocate John Dear names what's at stake in this premeditation:

> "If we do not tend to our nonviolence every day, we end up praying for God to bless our troops and kill our enemies. We will become modern-day persecutors of Jesus."[36]

This is exactly what I observed as the death threats started pouring in against me from fellow Christians on our Good Friday. And the attack finally came—but when I least expected it.

Angry curses and cutting insults were being shouted into my face. The man put me in a chokehold, and his thumbs thrust into my windpipe. I remember seeing his face full of enraged pain as he strangled me and shoved me backwards.

A year after the death threats started, this was actually happening. My heart was pounding. My spirit was spinning. And my voice was unhinged. I managed to resist raising my hands to attack back, but this was as far as my practice with Jesus took me. My shaming words only escalated the situation further.

But deliverance from evil came for both of us through an unexpected angel. It was my fiercely gentle wife, Lily.

Despite being much smaller in size, Lily inserted herself between our bodies and ducked under his arms as he strangled me. She could have easily been injured. But Lily was centered, spoke with calm composure, and persuaded him to step back. She peacefully separated us, engaged him in conversation, and completely deescalated the situation.

Lily embodied the radical fierceness of Jesus's nonviolence that day. I've never seen its paradox so personally or so profoundly before: pure gentleness and raw power embodied as one. Lily didn't raise her voice or raise her fist. She didn't threaten or attack. She held on and let go, resisting temptation and preventing us from crashing further into evil.

As we processed this traumatizing event, Lily told me how she stuck her landing. As our world was spinning, she was silently praying with Jesus, "Don't lead us into temptation but deliver us from evil." This prayer was her meditation in the most painfully dizzying moment of our life. And it enabled Lily to land and lead us through temptation into a shared deliverance.

I'm delighted to report that Lily and I and this brother reconciled nine months later. Jesus's practice of forgiveness took time to process but ultimately prevailed.[37] Together we've experienced the resilient healing Jesus promises us—even after the most traumatic event in our life. Amidst war and exile, the Neighbor-Love Movement continues its work today across boundaries of polarized identity. We are we.

Thankfully, not all of us will experience death threats and violent conflicts in war zones. But we will all face distressing troubles that tempt us to blackout, lose control, and unleash evil. We need to be ready, and Jesus presciently prepares us to be. This is the fierce flourishing that he offers us in his penultimate practice.

But even here, in this mature place of our spiritual adulthood, we may still secretly harbor this most addictive illusion—that our flourishing is ultimately about controlling power and prestige for ourselves. Many of us do to the end, even in our best work and greatest achievements.

And so there is still one last prayer for us to practice.

Practice Flourishing

We live in polarized societies in which insults, aggression, and violent conflict are increasingly normalized. Experiment with these exercises:

1. When you observe or experience escalating words, images, and situations, let them trigger you to pause and practice praying with Jesus, "Don't lead us into temptation but deliver us from evil." Retrain your instinct to react like Peter into a reminder to reach out your hand with healing power like Jesus and Lily.

2. If you receive death threats, turn them into invitations to bless enemy-siblings and pray for God's healing for all of us. Convert your aggression into premeditated energy for peace.

For more practices of enemy-love, visit iffglobal.org.

Chapter 7

Can You Let Go of Power and Prestige? Yours Forever

A Practice of Ultimate Surrender

> *"The man who makes another*
> *powerful ruins himself."*
> Niccolo Machiavelli[1]

> *"You will see for yourself that all things shall be well."*
> Julian of Norwich[2]

> *"You can have it all—my empire of dirt."*
> Johnny Cash[3]

Jesus's (Anti)climax: Great to Good

We've made it to the mountaintop—the seventh movement and final peak of Jesus's spiritual practice.

Getting here only takes thirty seconds if we just say the words. But living into this prayer's sevenfold maturity may take a lifetime. When Jesus taught it, he was thirty years old, a youth in his context. But this last movement bears the weighty wisdom and buoyant beauty of an elder nearing the end of life.[4]

What we find here may feel like an anticlimax. But it's utterly essential for our flourishing. It subtly strips off one last mask from our ego and invites us to look once more into prayer's mirror.

In it, we face our last troubling recognition: we can get to the end of our journey with Jesus and still secretly harbor the assumption that our flourishing is ultimately about controlling power and prestige for ourselves.

I believe this tenaciously entrenched assumption is what Jesus is testing for and challenging here at the end. With joyful defiance, he invites us to divest power and to pray to our Father, "*Yours* is the kingdom and the power and the glory forever" (Matthew 6:13).[5]

In 2001, Jim Collins published his wildly popular book *Good to Great*. "Greatness" is an ancient idol in culture and the shiny trophy of a triumphant life still today. As we saw in chapter two, the promise of a "greater" Germany moved millions of people to accept unspeakable evil.

But in the climax of Jesus's spiritual practice, we're taken in the opposite direction—from greatness back to goodness. We climb down the titanic mountaintop and return to the open river of our divine belovedness.[6]

These last words of Jesus, then, are a sacred sign-off. With them, he asks us one last question: *Can you let go of power and prestige?* This question probes into the secret chambers of our hearts. Have we finally accepted that we're loved by God and that God's kingdom is for all of us? Or are we still secretly grasping for our own ego and trying to prove that we're important?

Ultimate surrender is the final movement of our flourishing with Jesus. It's the ego death that we need to take us home, back to our beginning in divine belovedness.

But letting go of power and prestige is surprisingly difficult in practice.

KPG: Our Spiritual Pandemic

"Kingdom and power and glory," which I'll call KPG, names what many of us crave, secretly or not so secretly. Friedrich Nietzsche called it "the will to power." It's our drive to be in control and to prove our importance—perhaps even our superiority to others.[7] Consciously or not, we trenchantly believe that KPG is the endgame of life and the crown of our flourishing.

Of course, KPG goes by different aliases today. "Kingdom" gets called control, influence, ownership, sovereignty, winning. Our vernacular reveals the hidden violence in our egos and empires— "crushing it," "killing it," "dominating."

"Glory" gets called prestige, clout, celebrity, legacy, fame and fortune. It's the glow of our kingdom's greatness.

And power is the nuclear glue that binds them. Together, KPG offers us the specter of immortality. It's the addictive dopamine of impact and importance, and its possession momentarily makes us feel invincible and like we can live forever.[8]

When we look inside, KPG is not just the vice of villains unlike ourselves. Its claws are in all of us, though often unseen and so all the more powerful.

Perhaps you've observed a neighbor or friend or head of state—or yourself—passionately saying or doing some *thing*. But with time, it becomes clear enough that that thing isn't actually the *main* thing. What's really going on is something else: kingdom, power, and glory.

Consider these three examples.

A peace activist courageously stands against evils like poverty, racism, and war. He passionately invites people into the nonviolent way of Jesus. He's been arrested numerous times and nominated for the Nobel Peace Prize. And yet he repeatedly associates himself with globally powerful and prestigious celebrities. As he honors his "friends," it's hard not to hear another, suppressed whisper.

A thirty-something Christian consultant went off to New York City to serve "the kingdom of God" through business—a seemingly noble venture energized by Jesus's third practice. He worked in finance with some of the richest power brokers in America, and his excellence earned him promotions in a cutthroat environment. But a few years in, he was drug-addicted, burned out, and on the brink of total breakdown. After months of rehab, he was able to look back with honesty and admitted to me that he really went to NYC to "feel important," to get "clout," and to overcome his gnawing sense of "existential irrelevancy." The power trip consumed him.

A headline in a popular magazine ironically reads "The Christian Peacemaker Who Left a Trail of Trauma." The article unpacks how a leading mediator was hired to reconcile big-name churches, universities, and other institutions locked in conflict. But upon formal investigation, the pattern was clear: she herself consistently "abused her authority to protect those with power." Ten thousand students and many accolades later, we find out that her highly respected "ministry of reconciliation" was actually driven by power and prestige. The result was "a trail of trauma."[9]

In each case, these people were engaged in genuinely valuable work that can contribute to our flourishing, whether building businesses or making peace. We could insert any vocation here, from raising children to leading countries.

But we see how all this "great" work can be deeply rooted in our ego's desperate need to feel important, powerful, and perhaps even superior to others. And this addictive drive easily misleads us to use and abuse others—and ourselves—as we secretly seek after KPG.

This egocentric way of seeking significance inevitably leads to painful loneliness, insecure comparison, and ferocious competition. These, in turn, fuel gnawing anxiety, self-loathing, and relational conflict. Ultimately, the lust for KPG is the root of war. When fully metastasized, it mass-produces death, displacement, and destruction for millions of people. We see KPG raging in our world today.

But we don't need to look to war zones to see this. Another friend told me that he always felt like he needed to be "the most impressive person in the room." This need to impress others drove him into constant self-evaluation and a devouring loneliness.

Externally, he *was* impressive. In fact, he appeared to be living his dream: he was married with a high-paying job, a new baby, and a spacious home in a nostalgic neighborhood. But his depression grew into panic attacks, robbed him of sleep, and ravaged his ability to believe that anyone, including his wife, truly loved him. Thankfully, he had the courage to seek therapy, and this process has enabled him to accept himself like he cherishes his newborn baby.

The irony is rugged. Our addiction to KPG may drive us to succeed more and more, and others may be impressed by our greatness. But behind our invulnerable appearances, we find ourselves increasingly unsatisfied with life and far from flourishing.

Envy and pride—those feelings of being less or more than others—devour us and strangle the voice that says, "You are my beloved child; I delight in you." In its place, we hear those disintegrating voices of shame that whisper or roar, "You're never enough! You're better than them! You must win or you're nothing!" As psychiatrist Curt Thompson writes, "shame is committed to keeping us sick... it will not be satisfied until all hell breaks loose."[10]

KPG is the spiritual pandemic of our time.

With maddening regularity, yet another story emerges about yet another leader—"Christian" or otherwise—who built a massive church, or wrote best-selling books, or ran a global nonprofit, or struggled for peace on the front lines of war, or raised billions of dollars for groundbreaking innovation, or made breathtaking art. And then it's revealed that they ruled like a dictator, or abused people, or used funds to enrich themselves as they silenced their victims, or lied their way into power and money, or started a war because of personal ego.

In all the "great" work that they may have done, KPG was still the engine and operating system that fired their vision of "flourishing." And the results were predictable: burnout, corruption, and loss—trails of trauma.

This is surely one of the greatest paradoxes of being human: we can kill ourselves or kill others trying to prove that we're important. And yet we lose ourselves. This egocentric significance can't satisfy us, because it's a house built on the sinking foundation of envy, pride, and competition. The greater it gets, the more it collapses into insecurity, loneliness, and loss.

Again and again—at whichever pace and scale—KPG kills us. It's allergic to the mutual belovedness and larger belonging that we truly desire and always require to flourish.

Giving up KPG doesn't feel great, but it's good for us.

The Road Home

So here at the end, Jesus generously offers us one last opportunity to investigate our egos. He invites us to divest KPG and choose a more excellent way: to let go and name that the kingdom and power and glory are our Father's alone, now and forever. They are *Yours*—not mine or even ours.

This sacred sign-off may seem simple enough. But the vignettes above show that it's the mature work of a lifetime. We're all more heavily invested in KPG than we realize or care to admit. Earnestly letting go of it may feel like losing ourselves or dangling over death. Jesus described it with the cross, Rome's brutal technology of execution (Matthew 16:24).

Ultimate surrender is like uprooting mountains from our souls. But it shows us the road back home. In the end, it crowns our lives with nothing to prove and nothing to lose.

Saying *Yours* emerged out of the struggle of Jesus's own soul in his feverish moment of youthful temptation. Satan takes Jesus away to the mountaintop—that isolated peak of ambitious vision. He shows him "all the kingdoms of the world and their power and glory." With this panoramic fantasy flashing in his mind, Satan promises Jesus, "I will give you all of this if you will bow down and worship me. It will all be *yours*" (Matthew 4:8-9; Luke 4:7).

Jesus's response is brilliantly deviant and defiantly rebellious. He doesn't simply say no to Satan. He turns this satanic offer inside out and creatively converts it into a counter-confession of ultimate surrender to God. He climbs down the mountain. And then he teaches that wildly diverse crowd of people under Rome's imperial shadow to pray, "*Yours* is the kingdom and the power and the glory forever."

It was this prayerful practice that enabled Jesus to remain committed to divesting KPG as his fame exploded. We watch as Jesus renounces becoming a celebrity leader and bluntly declares, "I don't accept glory from humans… If I glorify myself, my glory means nothing." He calls the rich to give everything away to the poor—not to himself. And Jesus repeatedly challenges his followers to keep his movement secret, because the point wasn't ego and fame but God's presence and human healing.[11]

Unlike so many famous leaders, Jesus sticks his landing and resists being sucked into ego inflation, power games, and competition for greatness. At the end of his life, we witness a young but fully mature human being with nothing to prove and nothing to lose. As we've seen, Jesus proclaims forgiveness for his killers, promises paradise to a criminal, and confesses his trust in God's loving hands. This is true freedom and fierce flourishing.

Notice how Jesus's practice of saying *Yours* and divesting KPG unlocks two crucial possibilities for us still today.

First, kingdom and power and glory themselves begin to heal.

Our fantasies of imperial kingdoms gradually sober up and get exchanged for Jesus's inspiring vision of the kingdom that we explored in chapter three: countercultural love, mutual relationships, integrated healing, nonviolent witness, and everyday action. Our imagination, desire, and vocation start prepping for that global party in which everyone is welcome and "the least of these" are VIPs. Heaven and earth begin to gently overlap.

Power unplugs from our insecurity and self-importance, which can only lead to relationships of intimidation, competition, and exploitation. It converts into a cleaner energy that nurtures God's new we, encourages interdependence, and celebrates our shared dignity and security. What we truly love begins to reveal itself, and this flowering self creatively operates without the mutilating competition of the insecure ego. Power begins to heal, restore home, and transform death into life.

Divine glory melts through the glamorous greatness that we thought we needed. And we discover true joy, deep laughter, and the universal belonging of being loved, known, and at peace with one another, nature, and God. We're able to celebrate with others, and their happiness increases our happiness. We're able to grieve with others and empathetically trust that nothing will separate us from God's love. Jesus describes this divine glory as the resurrection that defeats death and shines with undying life.[12]

And so we return home—to our origin.

The One to whom we say Yours is the One that Jesus invites us to call our Parent. As we learn to let go, heaven opens afresh and we hear that healing Voice address us with our divine belovedness: *You are my beloved children; I delight in you.*

No longer are these words a mechanical mantra or half-believed hope. They become our breath and bone, our voice and vision. They wash through us with living water, and all things are illumined in their light.

We enter into a second childhood with new wonder, creativity, and belonging. We begin to remember with gratitude, to forgive with freedom, and to see enemies with love. Time is healed, and our present reintegrates with our past and future. Visions like Karin Sokel's of reconciliation with some of history's most notorious figures no longer strike us as absurd or offensive but full of wisdom, beauty, and hope.

We enter into this liberating paradox: in the end, letting go of KPG isn't self-deprecation or even ego death. It's perfect safety and the practice of a fierce flourishing that lives forever.

Nothing Is Lost

The first followers of Jesus rebelliously claimed that this is what happened when Jesus trusted God and died.

To be sure, there was a terrifying liminal period in which it simply seemed like murder was final and nothing more would happen. Absence—silence—grief—despair—pain. Holy Saturday is a haunting darkness that shadows all of human history. Each of us has felt like death is the end.

But that Sunday morning, Jesus's followers experienced something that changes everything. They witnessed that Jesus was alive again, raised from death's dungeon by our Father.

They saw him, touched his wounded body, and shared meals with him. They experienced that Jesus was completely himself and yet something entirely new: postdeath, transmortal, unkillably alive forever.

Recall that Jesus himself promised that this is what would happen because of who God is. He said, "The Father raises the dead and gives them life... No one can snatch them out of my Father's hand" (John 5:21; 10:29).

What this means for us is simple, but world-changing, if true. Violence doesn't win. Death isn't the end.

When we say *Yours* with Jesus, life flourishes *through* death and *out beyond* its reach into a new beginning for all of us. Our souls and bodies and relationships are healed with "the power of an indestructible life" (Hebrews 7:16). This was Jesus's final promise:

> "God will wipe every tear from [our] eyes. There will be no
> more death or mourning or crying or pain, for the old order
> of things has passed away. I am making everything new!"
> (Revelation 21:4-5)

Even victims of horrific suffering like Eyob are safe and fully at home in perfect healing. This is what I witnessed when I watched Eyob's final video message five years after his death: *Till you go to heaven—till you receive the reward from the hand of God—be strong and serve God intensely. May peace be with you.*

It's up to us to decide today whether Jesus's resurrection is worthy of our trust as we live our lives and face our own deaths.[13] But if this good news is true, it recasts letting go of KPG with a whole new light. What looks and feels like loss isn't loss at all but the prayerful pathway to new life:

Premeditated nonviolence isn't the naivety of fools; it's the prescient mind that anticipates eternity.

Forgiveness isn't weakness but the strength of an everlasting new beginning.

Daily bread isn't inadequate; it's actually enough and nourishes our transmortality.

Welcoming the kingdom of heaven doesn't leave us insecure and alienated; it's the only project that will never fail and the only triumph that humiliates no one.

Hallowing G-d's name isn't relativism disguised as reverence; it's preparation for the ultimate mystery of being held through death by the hands of I-Shall-Be.

Embracing our divine belovedness, even with enemies, isn't childish nonsense; it's the only childhood that always matures and never grows old.

When we says *Yours* with Jesus, then, death is not the triumph of evil and entropy. It becomes our sacred passage into God's new world.

The resurrection defies every disease, every dictator, and every agent of destruction that would dishonor our bodies. We will live again. Together we will experience the final healing that we have irrepressibly longed for in every tear, in all of our belly-deep laughter, in the ecstatic relief of every happy ending, and all of our experiences of beauty, acceptance, and joy.

"Nothing is ever lost."[14] All will be found.

A Strange Credibility

Saying *Yours* points through a paradox like a keyhole to eternity. When we're ready to let go with trust and to die with hope, we are most fully alive and ready to begin again. Our ego has undergone a death that isn't a destruction but a transformation that can never die.[15] *Yours* is the way back to that heaven-opening voice that speaks belovedness and delight to all of us without end.

For me, the strangest—and most oddly convincing—aspect of Jesus's resurrection is that he doesn't set up an earthly empire. The KPG model would lead us to expect this. In fact, it makes us feel like this is necessary for Jesus's resurrection to be real and reliable. Who defeats death and doesn't demonstrate it with undeniable publicity and invincible power?

But Jesus had actually let go of KPG and entered into a new quality of flourishing beyond this model's stunted imagination. With mirthful modesty, Jesus gives witness to this new life for a few weeks in rural Palestine. And then he simply disappears—into the next frontier of our journey with God.

The resurrected Jesus didn't need to kill his killers or install a regime. In fact, he didn't task his followers with getting even or imposing an ideology. As we saw in chapter five, Jesus simply proclaims peace, embraces the doubters, and restores the humiliated. He then sends this band of unlikely ambassadors out across every border of the empire to invite everyone everywhere to practice flourishing through *metanoia* and the baptism into our divine belovedness.[16]

It comes down to this: the resurrection of Jesus is either the world's most successful conspiracy theory or the climax of human flourishing. Those are the options.

What gives it credibility to me is that the witnesses of Jesus's resurrection were willing to die for it but unwilling to kill for it. Jesus's surrender of KPG had set them free. Their faith fueled a flourishing that was different from spiritual fantasy or religious fundamentalism. It enabled them to entrust their bodies to God and to embrace the unknown without fear.

The Romans called them "atheists" and attacked them for their heretical faith.[17] But Jesus's new atheism energized the first truly multi-ethnic, multi-lingual, multicultural, multi-gender, and multi-class movement in history.[18] These practitioners had room for the wildly diverse people that Jesus taught to call G-d *our* Father under shadows of Rome's bloody crosses.

Against all odds, Jesus's gospel movement outlived the violent Empire that had failed to end him. Ordinary people had discovered the hidden treasure of the kingdom of heaven, and this was far more precious to them than any fading kingdom, power, and glory.[19]

History's Best-Selling Stories

The most beloved stories of the last few war-torn generations strikingly retell the story of Jesus. It's what humans everywhere are wired for and gravitationally drawn into.

Of course, we live in a KPG-addicted world, and we rarely see our most lauded leaders in the halls of power practicing ultimate surrender. But we rebelliously repeat this story to ourselves in our most inspiring art and epic fiction.

These stories present entire universes locked in apocalyptic struggles for KPG. And as the world falls apart, Christ figures courageously surrender everything to save it. With profound insight, Peter Hartwig asks,

"Why would the God who hopes to be found by us not haunt us from within our own imaginations? God finds us precisely in the places where we're already wondering about God. It's in the stories we tell ourselves that we can see God already inside us, trying to call us Home."[20]

Take a fresh look at three familiar epics. *Spoiler alert:* The next three sections briefly unpack the endings of *Star Wars*, *The Lord of the Rings*, and *Harry Potter*.

Star Wars

An orphaned moisture farmer named Luke Skywalker and his ragtag friends forge a Rebellion against the totalitarian Empire. Meanwhile, Luke's unknown father Lord Vader—the ultimate patriarch figure— oversees the construction of a seemingly omnipotent weapon known as the Death Star.

As hope begins to vanish, the Empire's battle captain triumphantly declares, "This station is now the ultimate power in the universe!" It's the weaponization of KPG.

A countdown starts ticking away until the Rebellion will be obliterated with a single blast. Resistance feels futile, and the Empire's cosmic will to power seems unstoppable.

But Luke's friends have secretly stolen the design for the Death Star and discover a vulnerability in its hidden heart. As they desperately race to reach it, their tiny size ironically protects them from the Empire's massive Star Destroyers. At last, Lord Vader personally joins the battle and shoots down the Rebellion's fighters one by one.

The countdown to oblivion wastes away, and Vader menacingly trails his son. But Luke hears his mentor Obi-Wan Kenobi whisper wisdom from deep inside his heart: *Let go. Luke, trust me.* Luke takes a deep breath and navigates his mosquito-like ship into the core of the planet-like Death Star. He pulls the trigger and flies away.

We watch as Luke gasps with relief and the Death Star explodes into a ball of light. The Rebellion triumphs, and a new hope is born. At last, Luke hears his mentor whisper once more: "Remember: The Force will be with you always."[21]

The Lord of the Rings

J.R.R. Tolkien's *The Lord of the Rings* unfolds in a different world but follows a strikingly similar plot.

Evil spreads like a haunting shadow across Middle Earth as Sauron the Great frantically searches for his lost Ring of Power. This Ring is the "One Ring to rule them all"—the Master-ring of KPG that controls all others. If Sauron can recover it, the Dark Lord's power will become absolute, and Middle Earth will be ravaged by slavery and death.

The lost Ring reveals itself in the most seemingly innocent place: a birthday picnic enjoyed by two friends along a beautiful river. But when Deagol holds up his newfound treasure, Smeagol is seized with burning envy. He blacks out, murders his friend, and takes the Ring for himself. He then wipes his memory clean of this troubling recognition with a comforting denial: the Ring was really a birthday present from his grandmother and his by *right*.

The wise wizard Gandalf grimly observes that "neither strength nor good purpose" can last long under the Ring's "unwholesome power." It looks like a harmless, beautiful object that is easily handled and even destroyed. But Gandalf knows better and warns the Hobbit Frodo:

> "Its keeper never abandons it. At most he plays with the idea of handing it over to someone else's care—and that only at an early stage, when it first begins to grip."[22]

And *grip* it did. Smeagol, who becomes Gollum, is possessed by the Ring's addictive power, and his violence drives him into lonely

149

exile. Gollum grows to both love and hate the Ring, just like he loved and hated himself. He addictively needed the Ring to stay alive, even as it turned him into a monster. And so he jealously calls his ruinous KPG "My Precious."

But the Ring of Power betrays Gollum, like it betrays us, and changes hands yet again, yearning to return to its Master. *The Lord of the Rings* then becomes the quest of the small Hobbit Frodo and his ragtag Fellowship to return the Ring to the furious fires of Mount Doom—the only place where it could be unmade.

Along their treacherous journey, Frodo and his friends face many temptations to take an easier, faster road. These temptations all present themselves in the disguise of noble intentions for the greater good. But their secret heart is always the same: to wield the Ring's power for themselves.

In the end, Frodo and his loyal friend Sam risk everything and finally reach Mount Doom. But in the shadows of our world wars, Tolkien understood the addictive ferocity of power, and his story takes a shocking turn.

As Frodo's face glows with the fires that forged the Ring of Power, he doesn't have the strength to let it go. Like Gollum, the Ring's power had reached into his soul with its invisible fingers. It had become too precious to surrender—even as it sickened and terrorized him throughout his dangerous journey. At last, Frodo declares to Sam, "I do not choose now to do what I came to do... The Ring is mine!"

Everything seems lost as Sauron's servants race to recapture the Ring of Power. But with brilliant irony, salvation comes—at the hands of Gollum, who remained addicted to the Ring's power to the bitter end.

Gollum suddenly appears, hurls himself upon Frodo, and viciously bites off his ring finger. Drunk with glee, Gollum holds up the Ring, dances ecstatically, and loses his balance. He and the Ring on his finger fall into the consuming fire of Mount Doom, and he shrieks one last time—*Precious!*[23]

And that is how Sauron "the Great" is finally defeated: the Ring of Power is flung into the fire and destroyed forever—however unwillingly. Tolkien subtly reminds us that our flourishing follows a paradoxical path. It comes, not by capturing KPG, but by letting it go and returning home to an earth that's shared by diverse, interdependent creatures.

Harry Potter

J.K. Rowling's *Harry Potter* is the most recent retelling of Jesus's epic story. It's sold over 500 million copies and become the most successful book series in history, inspiring the imaginations of people everywhere.

Similar to Luke and Frodo, Harry Potter is an orphaned wizard boy who mysteriously survives the murder of his parents at the hands of the ruthless Lord Voldemort. Harry then becomes famous and known as "the Boy Who Lived."

Voldemort briefly vanishes but returns with a vengeance to destroy Harry and dominate the world. In their first showdown, Voldemort sneers at Harry with KPG's nihilistic thesis:

> "There is no good and evil. There's only power and those too weak to seek it."[24]

But the apparently powerless Harry survives yet again without cursing or casting any spell. His mentor, Professor Dumbledore, explains that the self-sacrificing love of his mother Lily lives on in his very skin. And so Voldemort couldn't bear to touch Harry's love-saturated body.

The story feverishly unfolds as the world grows darker and more deadly. The once-trusted government known as the Ministry of

Magic is infiltrated and rebrands itself with the KPG slogan "MAGIC IS MIGHT." A nostalgic ideology of racial superiority is weaponized against the weak and unwizard-like.[25]

Voldemort murders at will and unleashes his mob, declaring, "There is nothing worse than death." But Dumbledore, "the champion of commoners," fiercely protests:

> "You are quite wrong. Indeed, your failure to understand that there are things much worse than death has always been your greatest weakness."[26]

Still, Harry sinks deeper into pain, rage, and fear. Soon enough and with great irony, he and Lord Voldemort become "united in wanting the very same thing." They find themselves racing to possess the Elder Wand—the Deathstick or Wand of Destiny.[27] This wand was rumored to make its wielder invincible and master of Death. Controlling it appeared to be everything.

But Harry makes a surprising decision that makes all the difference: he abandons racing Voldemort for the powerful Elder Wand. Instead, he chooses a different road that requires him to face his pain, vulnerability, and mortality. Rowling writes that Harry "decided to continue along the winding, dangerous path indicated for him by Albus Dumbledore, to accept that he had not been told everything that he wanted to know, but simply to trust."[28]

At last, Harry faces Voldemort in the Forbidden Forest. But instead of raising his wand, Harry surrenders himself to save his friends. Voldemort raises the Elder Wand and screams the Killing Curse *Avada Kedavra*: "Let the thing be destroyed!"

But wildly beyond his own belief, the murdered Harry is not destroyed. Instead, he finds himself very much alive and with his murdered mentor Dumbledore in the King's Cross train station.

The befuddled survivor confesses to his mentor, "But I should have died—I didn't defend myself! I meant to let him kill me!" But Dumbledore cheerfully answers, "And that will, I think, have made all the difference."[29]

What Voldemort—and Harry himself—didn't understand is that "love, loyalty, and innocence... have a power beyond the reach of any magic." So the murdered yet mysteriously alive Dumbledore invites Harry into a whole new understanding of reality. He tells Harry,

> "Do not pity the dead, Harry. Pity the living, and, above all, those who live without love."[30]

At last, the resurrected Harry returns to face Voldemort one final time. But Voldemort's second Killing Curse rebounds on himself and takes his own life. Like Tolkien's Gollum, Rowling shrewdly shows how our addiction to power is ultimately suicidal; only the one who passes through King's Cross truly lives.[31]

Harry now holds the Elder Wand in his own hands with the promise of invincible greatness. The question crackles off the page with smoldering suspense: *What will the Boy Who Lived do with the Deathstick?*

Harry's response is remarkable. He says that he doesn't want it, snaps it in half, and throws it into the valley below. Harry shrugs, "That'll be the end of it," and the power of the Deathstick is broken forever.[32]

Strikingly, the triumphant Harry Potter doesn't go on to become the Minister of Magic or even the Headmaster of his beloved Hogwarts School. Instead, Harry abandons KPG, marries his girlfriend Ginny, and they raise children together.

After over a million words, Rowling ends history's best-selling story with three simple words: "All was well."[33]

With these words, Rowling echoes the words of one of history's most profound mystics, Julian of Norwich (1342-1416). In her

Revelations of Divine Love, Julian wrote,

> "And so our good Lord answered all the questions and doubts that I could raise, saying most comfortingly in this way, 'I may make all things well, I can make all things well, I will make all things well, and I shall make all things well; and you will see for yourself that all things shall be well.'"[34]

With extraordinary anticlimax, then, the heroic Harry chooses not to set up a new kingdom with power and glory. He breaks the cycle of trauma, raises a loving family, and "all was well."

That's everything, and I suspect it's the real magic of *Harry Potter*—the reason why this story speaks to millions of humans everywhere. It presents a world as power-hungry and heartbreaking as our own. But it shows that love is stronger than power. And this love leads us into a trust that no longer fears to die. What is truly terrifying is not death but a life addicted to power without love.

And when we surrender power for love, we safely pass through King's Cross, and we discover that we can live together forever. The climax of our flourishing isn't found in any Elder Wand or KPG. It's found in finally saying *Yours* and trusting that all will be well—even beyond our own belief and death itself.[35]

Our Future: Back to the Beginning

Here at the end, on the mountaintop of his spiritual practice and in the face of death, Jesus asks us, *Can you let go of power and prestige?*

This question excavates the story we truly trust and tell with our lives. Are we still living the old imperial story in which flourishing looks like winning power and prestige for ourselves—only to temporarily forget the terrifying fact that we're all dying? Or have we truly started over in Jesus's rebel story? This story defiantly celebrates that saying *Yours* and surrendering KPG is the climax of our flourishing. It's the King's Cross station that safely takes us through death and into everlasting life.

According to Jesus, saying *Yours* is the key to resurrection. When we say it and live it, death becomes a door. We discover that violence has an expiry date. Evil is undone, and entropy is not the end. The insecure, imperial order is slowly passing away. Great to good.

We hear once more that heaven-opening Voice whisper, *You are my beloved children; I delight in you—you can trust me.* And so we come home to the radical hope that our lives, the people we love, the ungrateful and wicked, the unwanted and left-for-dead—indeed, the whole human family, the entire earth, and the wildest reaches of reality—are all *Yours*.

And so we end where we begin—where all flourishing is founded forever.

This is Jesus's final invitation to us still today, with our shattering heartbreak and epic stories. Practice saying *Yours* with your life. Let go and surrender. Disbelieve the imperial propaganda and divest your stock in all KPG. Trust and don't worry about losing anything, much less kingdom or power or glory. Nothing is omnipotent except love.

Cherish being small, vulnerable, beloved children of G-d. We are *we*—and destined for resurrection. All will be well.

And *this* is *everything*.

Practice Flourishing

1. Spend some time uncovering the KPG that entices you. What forms of power and prestige ask for your attention, fill your imagination, and claim your desire?

2. Then surrender each one by praying, "Yours is the kingdom and the power and the glory forever." Choose to live a life whose value is found in our divine belovedness and resurrection hope rather than ego, ambition, and temporary winning in denial of death. This is the embodied story that takes us home.

Conclusion

A Billion Revolutions

"The revolution which was begun two thousand years ago by a disreputable Hebrew criminal may now have to be begun again by people equally disreputable and equally improbable."
James Baldwin[1]

Jesus was beautiful and radical—a massacre survivor, a friend of sinners, the embodiment of flourishing even through execution. Overcoming extraordinary pain and loss, Jesus's prayerful life launched the most successful revolution in history.

And it can continue with us today, however improbable and disreputable we may be, like Jesus himself.

In the prayer Jesus crafted, he addresses our most crucial questions and invites us to practice a spirituality that reimagines God and human flourishing. Two thousand years in, we're only beginning to understand its profound implications and who we can become together when we pay attention and pray with Jesus.

Like him, we are acutely familiar with pain, trauma, and anxiety. Our world aches with ecological crisis, increasing poverty, religious extremism, debilitating mental distress, and escalating conflict. New technology and explosive enmity threaten to unleash wars with unprecedented magnitudes of devastation. As individuals and societies, we continue to wrestle with those ancient-yet-existential questions of who we are, how to belong, and whether we have hope.

There is much at stake—for ourselves and our planet, now and for our future. As Curt Thompson reminds us, "Ultimately, we become what we pay attention to... Practice tends to make permanent."

What questions will claim our attention, and which answers will we practice with our lives?

Will we succumb to the false comfort of our entrenched habits and deadly addictions?

Or will we courageously choose to practice flourishing through our distress and the suffering of our world?

Wherever you are on the edge of faith, I invite you to pray with Jesus every day and to participate in a multi-billion-person movement that practices flourishing like this:

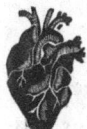

We open ourselves to God as our universal Parent. We embrace our divine belovedness and choose to see every other person as a sacred sibling in God's family, including our enemies. We are we.

We talk about G-d with radical reverence. We disavow religious hubris and cultivate deep humility in the face of holy Mystery.

We orient our dreams and energize our desires with prophetic imagination. We enlist in the kingdom of heaven that cherishes the most vulnerable, chooses mutuality, practices integrated healing, embodies nonviolent witness, and dignifies ordinary work.

We rescale our metric of enough with subversive simplicity. We break our daily bread and retrain our excessive appetites so trust, interdependence, and empathy can set a shared table for all of us, including our Eyobs.

We choose courageous healing. We confront our denial and confess our failures. We ask God to forgive us and forgive others so depolarization prevails and new beginnings of hope are unlocked.

We premeditate nonviolence before violence even begins. We befriend our bodies, acknowledge our vulnerability, process our distress with friends, and refuse to escalate conflict as we trust God to deliver us from evil.

We say Yours and divest our addictions to power and prestige. We embrace the ultimate surrender that takes us back home to our beginning in divine belovedness—and onward into the ever-living destiny of our universal belonging.

This is Jesus's invitation to all of us. This is his entire spirituality, carved in the beautiful grain of his own prayerful life.

When we practice these seven movements, flourishing is what happens in us and through us—as the unique persons that we are, in our relationships with others, spanning our diverse callings and cultures across our interconnected planet. Our vulnerability and vitality reintegrate. When we miss any of them, we atrophy an essential element of our humanity.

Of course, none of us will do this exactly the same way or get it perfectly right. The goal isn't imperial uniformity but expansive togetherness. Practicing this prayer with our lives will require us to face our distress and disrupt addictive habits, both as individuals and cultures.

But with patience, courage, and imperfection, our lives and world would undoubtedly flower like never before. Each of our daily decisions to practice with Jesus would amount to a personal revolution, rooted in our local lives but rippling out into the world toward larger transformation.

We dream of this in our most beloved stories, and we witness it in the people who inspire us. In this book, we've met Dietrich Bonhoeffer in Germany, David Hartsough in America, Hildegard Goss-Mayr in Poland, Nelson Mandela in South Africa, Dr. Denis Mukwege in Congo, and momma Itash and brother Eyob in Ethiopia. This flourishing is for all of us everywhere.

Today, around two and a half billion Christians claim to follow Jesus as the personal embodiment of God. Around two billion Muslims and Jews recognize Jesus as a holy prophet of God. Countless others are inspired by Jesus as a trusted spiritual guide. Together, these diverse people represent over one out of every two humans on planet Earth today.

I dream of even a small minority of these diverse people invisibly banding together every day to practice Jesus's prayer for our shared flourishing and so continuing the revolution that Jesus started.

Human dignity would buoyantly rise up, and othering would begin to heal.

Creative imagination would be fueled, and our competitive conflicts would find sustainable solutions.

Our neighbors in pain would be reprioritized, and we would learn to say to one another, "Seeing your face is like seeing the face of God"—every person, a Peniel.

Death would neither be denied nor weaponized. We would learn to face our mortality with honest grief and enduring hope. Amidst the ongoing tensions, tragedies, and aspirations of being human, we would live together with nothing to prove and nothing to lose.

I believe all of this was Jesus's dream when he designed this prayer and taught it to that wildly diverse crowd of people in the shadow of Rome's violent empire. This is how we—God's new we that sees even enemies as family—can build a shared home together in which nothing is lost, all will be well, and love never ends.

We are only just beginning to realize the revolutionary potential of Jesus's prayer.

So why pray?

To practice flourishing.

If this book has spoken to you, I'd love to start a conversation. You can contact me at andrew-decort.com and/or follow me on Facebook at andrew.decort.

How to (Re)read This Book
Throughout Your Life's Chapters

I hope you read this book however you want. But I encourage you to read it from start to finish. As I outlined in the Preparation, Jesus's prayer unfolds with a tightly integrated logic that moves from our origin in divine belovedness, into our mature flourishing, and onward into an everlasting future of new beginning with God and our sacred family. I don't want us to miss the rich, elliptical coherence of Jesus's spiritual practice.

But another way to (re)read *Flourishing on the Edge of Faith* is to focus on specific chapters in this book in particular chapters of your life. For example:

1. In times when meaning, self-worth, and identity are pressing on your mind, chapter one on God and our divine belovedness may be especially valuable.

2. Seasons where God feels a bit too familiar and dangerously certain may benefit from the radical reverence of chapter two. Yes, we should intentionally disrupt our false familiarity with God.

3. In a chapter focused on clarifying your dreams and vocation, chapter three on God's kingdom and prophetic imagination may be orienting and energizing.

4. Times of scarcity, insecurity, and anxiety may find fresh nourishment and trustful empathy in chapter four's exploration of our daily bread.

5. In the pain of failure and conflict, chapter five on forgiveness may offer healing comfort and positive challenge to unlock new beginnings of hope.

6. High-stress situations of escalating conflict and chaotic crisis can find premeditation for peace and courage for nonviolence in chapter six.

7. Mountaintops of ambition and success, as well as valleys of vulnerability and mortality, may find grounding sobriety and sustaining hope in chapter seven.

In Appendix 3, I provide questions for each chapter that cultivate deeper integration.

Appendix 2

Three Rhythms:
Praying and Breathing with Jesus

In my prayer life, I've found three fruitful rhythms for practicing flourishing with Jesus. Consider experimenting with them as you discover your own ways of praying with Jesus.

The first is to attentively pray through each of the seven movements all at once at the beginning of your day and then at other moments throughout your day. Make sure to go slow to keep your prayer thoughtful *practice* rather than slipping into thoughtless *habit*.

A second rhythm for praying with Jesus is to devote one day of your week to meditating on one of the seven movements in Jesus's prayer. This allows for greater focus, immersion, and internalization. For example, you might try this weekly rhythm:

1. Monday: Divine Belovedness
2. Tuesday: Radical Reverence
3. Wednesday: Prophetic Imagination
4. Thursday: Subversive Simplicity
5. Friday: Courageous Healing
6. Saturday: Premeditated Nonviolence
7. Sunday: Ultimate Surrender

A third way to pray with Jesus is to patiently practice one of these seven movements for several days, weeks, or months until it has saturated your consciousness. Once you've found that it's done the work it needs to do in your life, move on to another movement in the prayer. Use Appendix 1 for suggestions.

Whichever rhythm you follow, I encourage you to incorporate

breathing into your practice of prayer. Breathing prayer has become an incredibly powerful and peaceful practice in my life. Simply getting the words into our heads easily becomes a mindless habit and overly cognitive. Like playing sports and music, prayerful flourishing comes alive in our fully embodied selves.

In the ancient Hebrew imagination, breath is the vital gift of God that enlivens our enfleshed consciousness. Attentive breathing offers us the most primal rhythm of unceasing prayer and welcomes the Presence of God into the depths of our being. See Genesis 2:7 and John 20:22.

There's no right way to do this. But you might experiment with prayerfully inhaling and exhaling in the following way seven times or for a longer period of time in a centered moment of your day:

Inhale *Our* ....Exhale *Father*

Inhale *Hallowed* ....Exhale *be your name*

Inhale *Your kingdom* ....Exhale *come*

Inhale *Give us* ....Exhale *our bread*

Inhale *Forgive us* ....Exhale *we forgive*

Inhale *Deliver us* ....Exhale *from evil*

Inhale *Yours* ....Exhale *all power*

Experiment, enjoy, and continue practicing—especially when you experience distress in the process. Taking breaks is certainly important and part of the process. You'll know when as you practice with Jesus.

Study Guide: Questions for Conversation, Contemplation, and Conversion

The following questions are designed to help you reflect on what you've read, discuss it with others, and begin integrating Jesus's practice of flourishing into the evolving version of who you're becoming. That's what I mean by "conversion."

Preparation: The Spirituality of Jesus

1. Where are you on the spectrum of faith between "F*ck religion," "I don't know," and "I miss God"?

2. What assumptions, associations, or memories come to mind when you think of "the Lord's Prayer" or "the Our Father"? You may need to process and reset them in order to restart your practice of flourishing with Jesus.

3. What surprised you in Jesus's biography? How was he different or better than you imagined?

4. How might you experience Jesus's prayer in a new way if you engage it as a *practice* for your flourishing?

5. How might Jesus's prayer help you to reimagine and reenergize what flourishing actually means to you?

Chapter 1: Our Father

1. How do you typically address or imagine God, if you do at all?

2. Where are you on the spectrum of seeing Jesus's vision of our Father as too good to be true or a threat to your worldview?

3. What wounds in your life need to be explored in order to embrace that God is your Parent who says, "You are my beloved child; I delight in you"?

4. Who are you tempted to see as "other"—as unrelated or less than yourself? How might practicing calling God *our* Father expand your circle of identity and belonging into God's new we?

5. How might your life change if you started every day by addressing God as our Father? What self-rejection and/or rejection of others would slowly start to heal as you embrace God's love for you?

Chapter 2: Hallowed Be Your Name

1. Have you or someone you know had a hallowing experience of G-d like Jacob, Moses, Manoah, or Isaiah? What happened, and how did it affect your life?

2. Reflect on how you typically talk to and about "God." Does G-d's name too easily roll off your tongue in prayer, conversation, and/or arguments? Do you assume that "God" thinks like you do and/or wants what you want? Is G-d allowed to disagree with you and change you?

3. Who is your Esau, and what would it take for them to become your Peniel? Who do you need to tell, "Seeing your face is like seeing the face of God"?

4. Hitler promised to protect churches and restore family values in

Germany. In reality, he weaponized "God" to justify genocide. Where do you observe G-d's name being invoked but unhallowed in religion, culture, and politics today? Start by looking for examples in your own camp.

5. How might practicing hallowing G-d's name cultivate a deeper, if sometimes disruptive, personal and public flourishing?

Chapter 3: Your Kingdom Come

1. What do you want? What occupies your imagination and claims your desire?

2. Which of Jesus's five signs of the kingdom of heaven most inspires you? Which most challenges you?

3. Think about how you currently invest your time, energy, and resources. How might you re-energize what you already do by seeing it as service in God's kingdom?

4. How do you want to reimagine or change your life's work in light of Jesus's vision of God's kingdom? What empires might be colonizing your identity and loyalty?

5. Hartsough started answering his own prayer for God's kingdom to come on earth by challenging racial segregation rooted right at his lunch table. Is there an injustice in your society that especially opposes God's kingdom and cries out for your engagement?

Chapter 4: Give Us Our Daily Bread

1. Many cultures program us to believe that our basic needs like food and rest are unspiritual and shameful. Where are you in your journey of accepting and embodying that God cares about your daily bread?

2. Is there a place of uncertainty or anxiety in your life where you're working on trusting God? Do you have any professors of trust like Itash?

3. Depending on God for daily bread can be scary, especially when resources are scarce and God is calling you to take a risk for heaven's kingdom. Have you had an Independence Day when your fear and God's faithfulness collided? Are there any Eyobs in your life who show you the way of absolute dependence?

4. When you rescale "enough" with Jesus, are there surpluses in your lifestyle that you can reduce in order to nourish your empathy and share more of your daily bread with others?

5. Hunger and starvation haunt human history and remain devastating problems in our world today. Has God failed to provide? Or have we fabricated violent kingdoms and refused to share? How should we respond to human hunger in light of Jesus's teaching that God cares about our bodies and wants to give us *our* daily bread?

Chapter 5: Forgive Us as We Forgive Others

1. Where are you in your journey of accepting that God accepts you and wants to forgive your failures? Can you forgive yourself?

2. Who do you need to forgive and/or ask to forgive you? What failures may be especially difficult to confess but can unlock new beginnings of hope when you choose to do this?

3. What "us" are you part of that benefits from other people's exploitation? What do you want to do with your collective responsibility for "our sins"?

4. Are there people whose actions are so evil that they shouldn't be forgiven? What do you think about Jesus's decision to forgive

his murderers and the Polish survivors' decision to forgive their German neighbors after the Holocaust?

5. Does forgiveness require normalizing relationships with past abusers? Can we sincerely forgive others while also establishing healthy boundaries to prevent further abuse?

Chapter 6: Deliver Us from Evil

1. What are your triggers? When are you most vulnerable to fight or flight reactions?

2. The myth of redemptive violence—the idea that we can save ourselves with violence—is popular and powerful. Where are you on the spectrum between Peter's slashing sword and Jesus's command, "No more violence!"? How are you premeditating nonviolence in your life?

3. Peter thought he was expressing his loyalty to Jesus by defending him with violence. Where do you see religious nationalism crumbling to temptation like Peter today?

4. Jesus often retreated from conflict situations. But eventually, he accepted that it was his time to suffer and die. How do we discern when we're right to retreat and protect ourselves, and when we're called to sacrifice and suffer?

5. In extreme situations that endanger the most vulnerable, is violence ever a legitimate way to resist evil and love others? Or is this yet another pseudo-messianic, satanic temptation that escalates and unleashes evil? What alternative pathways to conflict transformation might we be foreclosing when we respond with violence? This takes us back to the question of how our imagination and desire are being shaped by the five signs of the kingdom of heaven.

Chapter 7: Yours Is the KPG Forever

1. What is your KPG?

2. *Star Wars*, *The Lord of the Rings*, and *Harry Potter* strikingly follow the plotline of Jesus's story: letting go of power, choosing surrender, and experiencing resurrection. Can you think of other stories or experiences in your own life that follow this pattern? How is God haunting us inside our imaginations?

3. Saying *Yours* might seem in tension with notions of stewardship and human responsibility. But how might actively surrendering KPG actually help us clarify our true vocations and reorient our work from greatness to goodness? How might saying *Yours* save us from slipping into distractions, burnout, and destructive messiah complexes?

4. Human KPG can be the most dangerous and hardest to detect when it's attached to "God." How can we cultivate a healthy critical discernment of religious KPG without surrendering to cynicism?

5. Humans are afraid of dying, and cultures around the world encourage us to live in denial of death. How might praying *Yours* with Jesus serve as a healthy practice of preparing to die and entrusting our mortality to God—now and throughout our lives until we walk through death's door?

Gratitude

This book is dedicated to the Peniels who have sourced and sustained my flourishing throughout my journey of following Jesus.

My mother Jane welcomed me into the world with divine belovedness and first taught me to pray with Jesus. I tell the story in chapter one of how she kept a lock of my baby hair as a reminder of her love for me before I even knew I was alive. Momza, your unconditional love has enabled me to trust my divine belovedness and to flourish with Jesus through the years of my life, especially the hardest ones. I love you.

Graham Smith was my first friend to invest in my writing. I'll never forget Graham handing me an envelope with $1,000 in it to catalyze a book project when I was a graduate student at UChicago. Graham, that money probably went to rent(!), but it deeply encouraged me, and I see *Flourishing on the Edge of Faith* as the flower of the seed you planted. You also encouraged me to start writing my weekly newsletter, *Stop & Think*, and developed my web platforms. Your spiritual honesty, professional creativity, generous empowerment, passion for mental health, and enduring commitment to me are precious beyond words. I love you.

David Schmidgall has been my beloved friend and personal pastor for over twenty years. Dave, when I embarked as a pioneer into a new frontier of my faith outside traditional church, you were always with me and trusted me when others rejected me. Your immersion in prayer and the practice of contemplation have profoundly shaped my life; you are my professor of prayer. You've also been the most consistent encourager of my writing along with Lily. I'll never forget sitting together at the Portrait Gallery in D.C. ("your writing is a stewardship issue") and then on the dock at Little Rocky Pond and hearing you say, "You have books inside of you." Your relentless encouragement and gentle feedback midwifed *Flourishing on the Edge of Faith* and significantly improved it. Thank you for your laughter in prayer and enduring friendship. *What I need is already here*. I love you.

Mark, Joelle, Jenna, and Ty have been the most extravagantly empowering champions of our work in Ethiopia and my life as a writer. Dear friends, your generosity has repeatedly blown Lily and me away and liberated us from our fear for a truly fierce flourishing with Jesus. Your confident trust, warm hospitality, honest conversation, wise counsel, evolving faith, and inspiring example of what flourishing can look like, in all of your own unique vocations, sustain me. Thank you for loving Lily and me so fiercely and so enduringly. You are our eucatastrophe; we love you.

Lily DeCort is my wife, my life partner, my best friend, my peacemaker, my healer, and my gift from heaven. Hod Fiker, your unconditional love, nourishing care, risky faith, gentle strength, courage to heal and grow, hunger for learning, and magnificent artistry have sustained and saved me again and again for the last fifteen years. You have opened windows into beauty, vulnerability, and the radical hope of heaven that reveal God's face to me and the gentle hands that hold me when I can't breathe. You embody divine belovedness and the integrated flourishing of Jesus's prayer like no one else I know. Jesus loves you, and I love you—*forever*.

I want to thank the board of the Institute for Faith and Flourishing (IFF): Liz Brown, Lily DeCort, Grant Hensel, James Hoey, and Dr. Steve Ivester in partnership with our brothers Dan Boyce and Joe DeCort III. You've wisely guided and generously empowered me to take risks, say yes to God, and "be the friend and brother of people everywhere, especially those who are exiles and pilgrims like myself."[1] I'm so deeply grateful for your enduring friendship and vital leadership. Special thanks to James for challenging me to write at a 5th grade reading level; apparently, I've made it to grade 7. :)

Special thanks to Grant for asking me the pointed question, "Are you willing to make your book less good by trying to do too many things?" Great to good!

Deep thanks to my beloved friend and brilliant partner in the Neighbor-Love Movement, Dr. Tekalign Nega. Tekalign, your trust, wisdom, and love encourage me to keep dreaming, even when it's different, difficult, and dangerous. I pray for you, Tehitena, Hesed, and Esset daily.

Deep thanks to every partner of the Neighbor-Love Movement through the Institute for Faith and Flourishing. Your generosity makes our work possible and fills me with endless gratitude. Learn more about NLM at nlmglobal.org and consider becoming a partner in our work at iffglobal.org.

Deep thanks to Jane and Joe DeCort for your generous hospitality and enduring love when Lily and I came home-away-from-our-war-torn-home; to the homeless brothers and sisters at Hesed House for showing me such kindness as I worked on this book; and to the Arnold, Shadid, and Solache families for sharing your cars, kids, and love with Lily and me so abundantly. Special thanks to Abigail Arnold for patiently giving me piano lessons and beautifully rebaptizing me in the art of practice.

Deep thanks to Dr. Duane Grobman, my spiritual director; Dr. Rich Hansen, my vocational coach; and Dr. John McPherrin, my therapist. Together, you've helped me begin, grow, grieve, heal, rest, end, begin again, and take the next step in my journey of flourishing. Warm thanks to Dr. Tom Schwanda and Jim Witt for your relentless prayer and encouragement; your words are on my desk. Special thanks to Dr. Curt Thompson for introducing me to the practice of divine belovedness in your healing book *The Anatomy of the Soul: Surprising Connections between Neuroscience and Spiritual Practices That Can Transform Your Life and Relationships*. This practice has saved my life.

Deep thanks to Provost Noah Toly for welcoming me so warmly and inviting me to present the vision of this book for the first time in public at Calvin University. *Pray, wait, and watch the impossible unfold.*

Enduring thanks to Dr. N.T. Wright who first unpacked Jesus's prayer for me and warmly welcomed me as an eighteen-year-old at his personal cloister in Westminster Abbey. Professor Wright, the first class that I ever taught was based on your book *The Lord and His Prayer*. My vision of Jesus and *Flourishing on the Edge of Faith* have been profoundly shaped by your research, writing, and teaching.

Astonished thanks to my champion-of-a-publisher Kate Schmidgall and her BitterSweet Collective. Kate, your unwavering belief in me, generous investment in this book, and elegant professionalism have shown me the more excellent way. You so beautifully embody the fierce flourishing of Jesus. February 11, 2022, will remain one of my happiest and holiest days—a blizzard of fresh powder.

Radical thanks to my brilliant editor at BitterSweet, Peter Hartwig. Peter, you gave me over 700 edits(!), gently killed my darlings to the happy end, and helped me make this book a lot better than it could have been without your creative insight, energizing conversation, and wonderful translations. Let's get to work on the next twenty books, shall we?

Warm thanks to Robert Winship for producing the audiobook of *Flourishing on the Edge of Faith*. Robert, your disarming kindness, genuine questions, and patient listening encouraged me and gave me confidence as I read these 65,000 words.

Grateful thanks to Obiekwe Okolo for his insightful design of the book cover, Holly Harris for her striking artwork to accompany each practice, and Greg Sitzmann for his elegant typesetting. You are masters of your craft, and the way you made your creative process a practice of this book's vision deeply inspired me.

The last shall be first, as Jesus said. I want to thank beloved friends—

many on the edge of faith—for stretching me into the fierce flourishing described in *Flourishing on the Edge of Faith*. You are my church. Some of you are mentioned in this book; all of you are in my heart—Andrew and Maryam Shadid, Anna Faulkner, Betty Kiros, Biruktawit Tagesse, Blakers, Professor Bruce Ellis Benson, Camila Katherine, Christopher Upham, Colton Bernasol, Professor Daniel Master, David Ellis, David Johnson, David Robinson, Eleanor Pearl, Eden Gelan, Elias Schulze, Evan Hunter, Eyob†, Eric Hoskins, Ermias Zeleke†, Pastor Ermias Amanuel, Hallelujah Lulie, Hannah Gross, Isabell Reichert, Katie Robinson and Evangeline Smith, Kidus Dessalegn, Jason DeCort, Jason Ferenczi, Jawar Mohammed, Professor Jean-Luc Marion, Professor Jean Bethke Elshtain†, Leo Jorge, Liliana Jane, Lydia Ruth, Professor Matthew Robinson, ABD Matthew Vega, Michael Liu, Muluken Nega, Philipp Schütz, Ransom Reul Andrew, Roger Sandberg, Sean Lyon, Shane McShane, Shiferaw Yinessu, Dr. Solomon Dersso, Susan Shadid, Suzanne and Keith Ross, Tanner Gesek, Thomas Bernasol, Tobias Messner, Tom Gardner, Wudenesh Tilahun and Itash, Valentina Jane, Professor William Schweiker, Yonas Urgecha, Eleni Atlaw, Esayas Ayelew, Naomi, Noli, Naodi, Nazri, Lishan John, Jazzy, Ababi, Zewdnesh, Ezra, and Lily's beloved mother Tsegireda†.

You are all Peniels for me. Together, you save my faith that we are all we and destined for flourishing in God's love forever.

Seeing your face is like seeing the face of God

Endnotes

Preface: *Flourishing on the Edge of Faith*

1 The Killers, "Bling," Track 4 on *Sam's Town* (Island Records, 2006).

2 I share these stories with my friends' written permission.

Preparation: *The Spirituality of Jesus*

1 Henri Nouwen, *Spiritual Direction: Wisdom for the Long Walk of Faith* (New York, NY: HarperCollins, 2006), 151.

2 My interpretation of Jesus has been profoundly influenced by the scholarship of New Testament scholar N.T. Wright. See his *The Lord and His Prayer* (Grand Rapids, MI: Eerdmans, 2014) and *Jesus and the Victory of God* (Minneapolis, MN: Fortress Press, 1996).

3 See James Cone, *The Cross and the Lynching Tree* (Maryknoll, NY: Orbis, 2013). As I'll describe in chapter six, the Neighbor-Love Movement was born in part out of seeing the images of a man getting publicly lynched in Shashemane, Ethiopia.

4 See Howard Thurman, *Jesus and the Disinherited* (Boston, MA: Beacon Press, 1996), 18: "Christianity was born in the mind of this Jewish teacher and thinker as a technique of survival for the oppressed."

5 Hannah Arendt, *On Revolution* (New York, NY: Viking Press, 1965), 76-77.

6 See Thomas Keating, *The Human Condition: Contemplation and Transformation* (Mahwah, NJ: Paulist Press, 1999).

7 Thomas Davenport and John Beck's *The Attention Economy* (Cambridge, MA: Harvard Business Press Review, 2001) was a groundbreaking study arguing that attention is the most precious commodity in today's information-overloaded world. From this perspective, prayer asks for our most precious possession and promises to transform it.

8 Curt Thompson, *The Soul of Shame: Retelling the Stories We Believe about Ourselves* (Downers Grove, IL: IVP Books, 2015), 48.

9 I explore pain and prayer in my essays "Disappointment with God," August 12, 2019 at andrew-decort.com and "Groaning: Love in Pain," *Cultivare*, Issue No. 20, April 2022 at cultivare.net.

10 Amanda Gorman, *Poems: Call Us What We Carry* (New York, NY: Viking, 2021), 43.

11 Brother Lawrence, *The Practice of the Presence of God*, translated by John Delaney (New York, NY: Image Books, 1977), 41, 47.

12 When I was a graduate student at the University of Chicago, my roommate Brian practiced Jesus's prayer every time he peed. Hearing Jesus's words and the splashing of the toilet together was a hilarious and wonderful reminder to pray with Jesus throughout the day. I think Jesus would have laughed and celebrated Brian's practice.

13 The idea of capacities is rich and essential to human flourishing. For a profound introduction, see Martha Nussbaum, *Creating Capabilities: The Human Development Approach* (Cambridge, MA: Harvard University Press, 2013).

14 Martin Luther King Jr., *Strength to Love* (Minneapolis, MN: Fortress Press, 2010), 138.

15 When Jesus taught his prayer, he warned against two forms of praying that can't lead us to flourishing (Matthew 6:5-8). The first tries to impress others with eloquent words to be heard by others. Prayer becomes a religious ritual for relieving our distress by gaining status in our community. The second tries to manipulate God with many words. Prayer becomes a magical ritual for relieving our distress by trying to control God. Jesus warns that both are dead-ends.

16 For a profound study of addiction, see Gabor Maté, *In the Realm of Hungry Ghosts: Close Encounters with Addiction* (Berkeley, CA: North Atlantic Books, 2010).

17 Curt Thompson, *The Soul of Shame: Retelling the Stories We Believe about Ourselves* (Downers Grove, IL: IVP Books, 2015), 90.

18 Andy Crouch's *Strong and Weak: Embracing a Life of Love, Risk, and True Flourishing* (Downers Grove, IL: InterVarsity Press, 2016) insightfully shows how weakness and strength are both necessary and must be integrated for authentic flourishing.

19 I unpack a more rigorously philosophical and theological vision of flourishing in my chapter "On Human Flourishing: A Call for Public Responsibility in Contemporary Ethiopian Christianity," in *The Role of the Church in Fostering Democracy and Sustainable Human Development*, eds. Samuel Deressa and Josh de Keijzer (Fortress Press, 2020), 37-63.

20 Martin Luther King Jr., *Strength to Love* (Minneapolis, MN: Fortress Press, 2010), 2.

21 Both passages are quoted in Andrew DeCort, *Bonhoeffer's New Beginning: Ethics after Devastation* (Lanham, MD: Fortress Academic/Lexington Books, 2018), 168 and 185.

22 Buddhist scripture describes understanding and practice as the two wings of a bird that together enable flight. This integration of mind and body, past and future, is the feathered flourishing that Jesus offers us with his spiritual practice of prayer. See Donald Lopez, Jr (editor), *Buddhist Scriptures* (New York, NY: Penguin Classics, 2004), 21-22 and 373.

I'm reminded of Emily Dickinson's beautiful line, "Hope is the thing with feathers." See *The Poems of Emily Dickinson*, edited by R.W. Franklin (Cambridge, MA: Harvard University Press, 1999), poem 314.

23 We can map Jesus's prayer onto seven core stages or dimensions of human development: (1) birth and being held in love (Our Parent); (2) learning to talk (Hallowed be Your name); (3) learning to walk and enact our desire (Your kingdom come); (4) nourishing ourselves and sharing our resources with others (Give us today our daily bread); (5)

managing our waste and resolving conflict (Forgive us as we forgive others); (6) confronting our aggression and building resilience under distress (Don't lead us into temptation but deliver us from evil); (7) and trustingly letting go of power in the face of death (Yours are the kingdom and the power and the glory forever). From another lens, Jesus's prayer addresses seven core disciplines and domains of human life: (1) theology, (2) communication, (3) politics, (4) economy, (5) conflict, (6) evil, and (7) (im)mortality.

24 My first book focused on the ethics of making new beginnings in the thought of Nazi-resister Dietrich Bonhoeffer. See Andrew DeCort, *Bonhoeffer's New Beginning: Ethics after Devastation* (Lanham, MD: Lexington Books/Fortress Academic, 2018).

25 See Matthew 5:19 and 7:24-27.

26 The Yale legal scholar Jack Balkin observes, "In almost... every community that organizes itself around a set of practices and beliefs inherited from the past, a return to origins and to basic principles is a standard method for urging reform, and especially radical reform." Radical reform is very much the aspiration of this book. See Jack Balkin, *Living Originalism* (Cambridge, MA: Harvard University Press, 2014), 97.

Chapter 1
Who Is God? Our Parent

1 J.K. Rowling, *Harry Potter and the Deathly Hallows* (New York, NY: Scholastic, 2009), 739.

2 Henri Nouwen, *The Inner Voice of Love: A Journey through Anguish to Freedom* (New York, NY: Doubleday, 1998), 8

3 In her beautiful novel *The Dean's Watch*, Elizabeth Goudge tells the story of a Dean of an old cathedral in England. As he speaks with the watchmaker Isaac Peabody, the Dean says, "We always tend to make God in our own image, and your father was perhaps a man of stern rectitude." The Dean was right: Peter's father had brutally abused him. As Peter begins to cry, the Dean continues, "And no doubt as a boy you hated God as much as you hated your father. But your hatred, Mr. Peabody, God took into His own body that it might die with Him." Peter responds by insisting that he no longer believes in God. But the Dean replies, "I wish I could believe you. I should be thankful to believe you had parted company with the God of your boyhood. But I fear he is with you still in a darkness that shadows your mind at times. Disbelieve in him, Mr. Peabody. Believe instead in love. It is my faith that love shaped the universe as you shape your clocks, delighting in creation." The Dean's fierce wisdom—to disbelieve in the "God" of our abusive pasts and to believe instead in love—beautifully captures how Jesus reintroduces us to God as our Father. See Elizabeth Goudge, *The Dean's Watch* (Peabody, MA: Hendrickson Publishers, 2012), 275.

4 The first and foundational chapter of the Bible teaches that our Creator is equally reflected in both women and men—a plurality that embraces and exceeds human gender (Genesis 1:26-27). The profound medieval mystic Julian of Norwich developed this insight and wrote that God is "our true Mother." She saw God's Motherhood revealed in God's act of creating us, hugging our humanity, and sharing a love that stretches beyond our human-made boundaries. See Julian of Norwich, *Revelations of Divine Love*, translated by Barry Windeatt (New York, NY: Oxford University Press, 2015), 129.

5 The story of Jesus's early childhood is told in Matthew 2.

6 See Matthew 17:5; Mark 9:7; Luke 9:35; 2 Peter 1:17; John 12:28.

7 Quoted in Brian Muraresku, *The Immortality Key* (New York, NY: St. Martin's Press, 2020), 1. See Stephen Ross, et al., "Rapid and Sustained Symptom Reduction Following Psilocybin Treatment for Anxiety and Depression in Patients with Life-Threatening Cancer: A Randomized Controlled Trial," *Journal of Psychopharmacology*, vol. 30, no. 12 (December 2016): 1165-80. Dinah's experience is common in this research.

8 Personal correspondence from Simon Howard on January 20, 2022. Shared with permission.

9 Henri Nouwen, *Life of the Beloved: Spiritual Living in a Secular World* (New York, NY: Crossroad Publishing, 1993), 26. Are we right to hear what God says to Jesus and apply it to ourselves? This is exactly what Jesus's student John did. He wrote, "See what great love the Father has lavished on us, that we should be called children of God! And that is what we are!" (1 John 3:1).

According to a later John, this is essentially the practice of contemplation: "contemplation is naught else than a secret, peaceful and loving infusion from God, which, if it be permitted, enkindles the soul with the spirit of love." See St. John of the Cross, *Dark Night of the Soul* (Mineola, NY: Dover Publications, 2003), 27.

10 The Essenes, an apocalyptic Jewish sect contemporary with Jesus, taught that non-retaliation toward enemies would motivate God to punish them even more severely in the final "Day of Vengeance" (Community Rule 10:17-20). Here nonviolence is a spiritual stab-in-the-back.

The Roman philosopher Seneca, who was also a contemporary with Jesus, advocated ignoring enemies as an expression of moral superiority and apathy toward them, like an elephant disregarding a barking dog. Seneca called this "the most contemptuous form of revenge" (*On Anger* 2:32).

Aristeas, a Jew living in Egypt a few generations before Jesus, thought that showing "generosity" toward opponents might "win them over to what is right and to what is advantageous to us" (Aristeas 227). Here benevolence toward enemies has an evangelistic and strategic purpose: it can earn God's favor and access to power. This idea is reflected in other Jewish writings at the time, which makes sense in light of Jews' minority status in hostile societies.

None of these forms of non-retaliation is primarily concerned for the enemy and their wellbeing. *Loving* the enemy wasn't part of the picture. I further unpack Jesus's groundbreaking ethics of enemy-love in my essay, "Love Your Enemy" at iffglobal. org. This webpage has three other resources that may be helpful for our practice: (1) a "Self-Awareness Inventory," (2) "35 Practices of Enemy Love," and (3) an "Enemy-Love Reading List."

11 Michael Pollan, *How to Change Your Mind: What the New Science of Psychedelics Teaches Us About Consciousness, Dying, Addiction, Depression, and Transcendence* (New York, NY: Penguin Press, 2018), 71.

12 Nelson Mandela, *Long Walk to Freedom* (New York, NY: Bayback Books, 1994), 462.

13 See Larry Siedentop, *Inventing the Individual: The Origins of Western Liberalism* (Cambridge, MA: Harvard University Press, 2017) and Erica Chenoweth, *Civil Resistance: What Everyone Needs to Know* (New York, NY: Oxford University Press, 2021). Chenoweth's data is extensive, ranging from 1900 to 2019 and looking at 627 cases. She demonstrates that nonviolent civil resistance is twice as effective as violent methods for bringing sustainable change. It's always successful when just 3.5 percent of a society's population commits to a nonviolent campaign. Chenoweth doesn't discuss Jesus in her research, but Jesus introduced the spiritual vision and basic practices for this counter-intuitive way of confronting injustice and catalyzing change. See Walter Wink, *Jesus and Nonviolence: A Third Way* (Minneapolis, MN: Fortress Press, 2003).

14 Jesus's story is found in Luke 15:11-32. For further exploration of this profound story, see Henri Nouwen, *The Return of the Prodigal Son: A Story of Homecoming* (New York, NY: Image, 1994) and Kenneth Bailey, *The Cross and the Prodigal Son: Luke 15 through the Eyes of Middle Eastern Peasants* (Downers Grove, IL: IVP Books, 2005).

15 Over coffee in a slum in Addis Ababa, I painfully remember my friend Itash telling me about how her daughter Wude was partially paralyzed by bone tuberculosis. Out of desperation to cover her medical expenses, Itash asked her dad for her inheritance before his death. Sadly, he was so offended by her request that he cut her out of his life and gave her nothing, even after he died. Itash's painful experience illustrates the truly radical love of the father in Jesus's story.

16 The command to kill rebellious children is found in Deuteronomy 21:18-21. The father's rebellious declaration is found in Luke 15:23.

17 See Luke 16:15 and Matthew 7:21; 10:33.

18 The command to kill violators of the Sabbath is found in Numbers 15:32-36. Jesus's revisionary statement is found in Matthew 12:12.

19 See Matthew 10:30 and Luke 21:18. Jesus's vision is probably echoing back to Psalm 40:13 and 69:5 where the Hebrew poet reflects on their vulnerability and mortality.

20 You can find Jesus's statements in Matthew 18:10, 14; 10:29; 26:39-53; Mark 14:36; and Luke 22:43.

21 I'm referring to how God holds Jesus through the asphyxiating death of crucifixion. But I'm also alluding to the murder of George Floyd under the knee of a police officer on May 25, 2020. God is able to undo this grave injustice, and ultimately "the stone that the builders rejected" will become the cornerstone, as Rev. Sharpton said in his funeral eulogy for Floyd on June 9, 2020.

22 See J. David Schloen, *The House of the Father as Fact and Symbol: Patrimonialism in Ugarit and the Ancient Near East* (Boston, MA: Brill Publishers, 2001).

23 For a helpful book on the meanings and limits of "patriotism," see Martha Nussbaum, et. al., *For Love of Country: Debating the Limits of Patriotism* (Boston, MA: Beacon Press, 1996).

24 Martin Luther King Jr., *"Playboy Interview,"* in *A Testament of Hope: The Essential Writings and Speeches of Martin Luther King Jr.*, edited by James Washington (New York, NY: HarperOne, 1991), 359.

25 Jesus condemns abuse in Matthew 18:6-9, Mark 9:42-50, and Luke 17:1-5. I discuss Jesus's statements in my essay "Jesus's Condemnation of Abuse" on March 30, 2019, at andrew-decort.com.

26 James Baldwin, *The Fire Next Time* in Toni Morrison (editor), *James Baldwin: Collected Essays* (New York, New York: The Library of America, 1998), 314.

27 For a fiercely honest and critical discussion of Christian patriarchy, see *Christianity, Patriarchy, and Abuse: A Feminist Critique*, edited by Joanne Carlson Brown and Crole Bohn (New York, NY: Pilgrim Press, 1990).

28 This subversive vision of God as liberating Father is deeply rooted in Jesus's Hebrew tradition as we'll see in chapter two. The first time God is described as a Father in the Bible is when God hears the devastated groaning of enslaved people and declares to Pharaoh, "Let my children go!" (Exodus 3:7; 4:22-23; see Jeremiah 31:3, 8-9). Because God loves and listens, God liberates. Interestingly, this liberation movement is launched by rebellious women who refuse to obey their ruler's murderous orders (Exodus 1:15-21). Jesus's movement was also funded and supported by a collective of powerful women (Luke 8:1-3).

29 Thich Nhat Hanh, *Essential Writings* (Maryknoll, NY: Orbis Books, 2001), 130. Rev. Barbara Holmes explores this in her podcast "The Cosmic We" at cac.org.

30 The Ten Cities were infamous for their Greco-Roman culture and worship of the foreign gods.

31 In case we miss the point, Matthew, a biographer of Jesus, tells us that as soon as Jesus finished this teaching, he immediately focused his attention on (1) a leper, then (2) a Roman commander, then (3) a feverish woman, then (4) two men with mental illness, then (5) a paralyzed man, then (6) a group of "sinners" and cultural traitors, then (7) a woman with uncontrollable bleeding, then (8) a dead child. Matthew wants it to be unmistakable that Jesus was creating a new family out of the most unlikely and unliked people. See Matthew 8-9.

32 Nelson Mandela highlighted the great power of this little word "we." Reflecting on his experience in prison, he wrote, "We were not even permitted to use the word we." South Africa's jailers understood that the solidarity of "we" was dangerous to their system of racism and oppression. See Nelson Mandela, *Long Walk to Freedom: The Autobiography of Nelson Mandela* (New York, NY: Bayback Books, 1994), 395.

33 Quoted in Tracy Kidder, *Mountains Beyond Mountains: The Quest of Dr. Paul Farmer, a Man Who Would Cure the World* (New York, NY: Random House, 2009), 294.

34 Desmond Tutu, *No Future Without Forgiveness* (New York, NY: Doubleday, 1999), 109, 265.

35 Donald Lopez Jr (editor), *Buddhist Scriptures* (New York, NY: Penguin Classics, 2004), 524-525.

36 The texts that have most shaped my interpretation of Islam include Abdulaziz Sachendina, *The Islamic Roots of Democratic Pluralism* (New York, NY: Oxford University Press, 2001), Yaser Ellethy, *Islam, Context, Pluralism and Democracy: Classical and Modern Interpretations* (New York, NY: Routledge, 2014), and Oddbjørn Leirvik, "Aw qāla: 'Li-

jārihi': Some Observations on Brotherhood and Neighborly Love in Islamic Tradition," *Islam and Christian–Muslim Relations* (2010), 21:4, 357-372.

37 In a letter from prison, Paul of Tarsus, one of the original champions of Jesus's movement, wrote that Jesus "preached peace to you who were far away and peace to those who were near." Jesus's purpose was "to create in himself one new humanity" and "to put to death the hostility" between people who saw themselves as separate families. Jesus tore down "the dividing wall." In light of Jesus's prayer, it's no surprise where Paul lands this summary of Jesus's mission: "through him we both have access to the Father by one Spirit" (Ephesians 2:14-18).

38 Julian of Norwich, *Revelations of Divine Love*, translated by Barry Windeatt (New York, NY: Oxford University Press, 2015), 165.

Chapter 2
How Should We Talk About God? Hallowed

1 From Hitler's "Radio Broadcast" on October 14, 1933 in *Adolf Hitler: Collection of Speeches* 1922-1945 on page 148 of the PDF available on the Internet Archive website at tinyurl.com/HitlerRadioBroadcast.

2 Dietrich Bonhoeffer, *Creation and Fall: A Theological Exposition of Genesis* 1–3, edited by John W. de Gruchy, translated by Douglas Bax (Minneapolis, MN: Fortress Press, 1997), 29-30.

3 Meister Eckhart, *Selected Writings* (New York, NY: Penguin Classics, 1994), 236-237.

4 From Hitler's "Radio Broadcast" on October 14, 1933 in *Adolf Hitler: Collection of Speeches* 1922-1945 on page 148 of the PDF available on the *Internet Archive* website at tinyurl.com/HitlerRadioBroadcast.

5 From Hitler's "Speech before the Greater German Reichstag" on January 20, 1939 available on the *German History in Documents and Images* website at ghdi.ghi-dc.org. See David Livingstone Smith, *On Inhumanity: Dehumanization and How to Resist It* (New York, NY: Oxford University Press, 2021), 6.

6 See Eberhard Bethge, *Dietrich Bonhoeffer: A Biography*, revised edition (Minneapolis, MN: Fortress Press, 2000), 601.

7 Gerhard Kittel, editor of the still-authoritative *Theological Dictionary of the New Testament*, is a disturbing example. See Robert Ericksen, "Theologian in the Third Reich: The Case of Gerhard Kittel," *Journal of Contemporary History*, 12 (1977, 3): 595–622.

The quotation comes from a lecture course Bonhoeffer gave at the University of Berlin in 1933, which is published as Dietrich Bonhoeffer, *Creation and Fall: A Theological Exposition of Genesis 1–3*, edited by John W. de Gruchy, translated by Douglas Bax (Minneapolis, MN: Fortress Press, 1997), 29.

8 As I write, Vladimir Putin has launched a war against Ukraine. In Moscow, Archbishop Kirill, leader of the Russian Orthodox Church, has defended the war as the work of "God." The playbook of religious oppression is uncreative. See Scott Kenworthy, "Why Is Russia's Church Backing Putin's War?" *The Conversation*, March 21, 2022 at theconversation.com.

9 Amanda Gorman, *Poems: Call Us What We Carry* (New York, NY: Viking, 2021), 63.

10 Hitler recruited children to join his movement from the very beginning, and he established his organization Hitler Youth in 1926. One of the recruitment tools that Hitler used was a spin-off—really a total rewriting—of Jesus's prayer, which focused entirely on Hitler. In place of the prayer "Hallowed be your [God's] name," Hitler substituted, "Your [Hitler's] name makes the enemy tremble." Hitler replaced hallowing with hatred. See "Innocence and the Third Reich: How Propaganda Influenced the Hitler Youth—Primary Sources" at propagandaonhitleryouth.wordpress.com/primary-sources/.

11 John of the Cross, *Dark Night of the Soul* (Mineola, NY: Dover Publications, 2003), 4.

12 For example, see Genesis 27:20; 28:21-22; 31:3, 9.

13 These stories are told in Genesis 25:21-34 and 27:1-33.

14 Unless otherwise noted, all translations from Hebrew scripture in this section use Robert Alter's *The Five Books of Moses: A Translation with Commentary* (New York, NY: W.W. Norton & Company, 2004).

15 See Genesis 31:5-21.

16 See Genesis 32:7-12.

17 See Genesis 32:22-32.

18 Here I use *The Translation of the Jewish Study Bible* (New York, NY: Oxford University Press, 1999).

19 See Emmanuel Levinas, *Totality and Infinity*, translated by Alphonso Lingis (Pittsburgh, PA: Duquesne University Press, 1969), 66, 197.

20 Jesus does exactly the same thing in his story about the prodigal son and his loving father in Luke 15. He provocatively pictures the despised Esau as Peniel or the Face of God.

Notice these unmistakable similarities. (1) Both Jacob and the younger son take their fathers' inheritance improperly and run away. (2) Both get into serious trouble far from home. (3) Both return home desperate for mercy. And then (4) Esau and the father respond identically: "Esau [a] ran to meet Jacob and embraced him; he [b] threw his arms around his neck and [c] kissed him" (Genesis 33:4) / "His father saw him and was filled with compassion for him; he [a] ran to his son, [b] threw his arms around him and [c] kissed him" (Luke 15:20).

Jesus takes Esau as the model for the God-personifying father. In later Hebrew scripture, God had declared, "I hate Esau" (Malachi 1:3). But Jesus subtly redeems Esau as Peniel.

We see that Jesus was a subversive interpreter of Scripture who centered love. This was a major reason why he was labeled a heretic and condemned. The religious leaders found Jesus's love-centering revisions and innovations intolerable. But Jesus insisted that even the Bible itself falls apart without loving our neighbors (Matthew 22:4). And so Jesus reimagines Esau as no longer God-hated but God-embodying.

21 See Genesis 35:29.

22 Moses's origin story is told in Exodus 1-2.

23 The story of Moses's encounter with God is told in Exodus 3.

24 God is described like this in Exodus 3:7-10 and 4:22.

25 These quotations come from my lecture notes from Professor Michael Fishbane's course "Introduction to Hebrew Bible" at the University of Chicago, recorded on October 9, 2006.

26 Dietrich Bonhoeffer, "The History of Twentieth-Century Systematic Theology" in Dietrich Bonhoeffer, *Ecumenical, Academic & Pastoral Work: 1931–1932*, edited by Victoria Barnett et al., translated by Anne Schmidt-Lange, et al. (Minneapolis, MN: Fortress Press, 2012), 229-30.

27 See James Cone, *God of the Oppressed*, revised edition (Maryknoll, NY: Orbis, 1997), 65. Centuries later, God declares through the prophet Hosea, "I am Not-Your-I-Am/ Yahweh." Here God protests against Israel's religious invocation of God's name but disregard for God's just character (Hosea 1:9; 12:1-9).

28 Biblical translations in the remainder of this chapter are from *The Jewish Study Bible*.

29 Abraham Joshua Heschel, *The Prophets* (New York, NY: Harper Perennial Modern Classics, 2001), 8.

30 See Isaiah 1:10-17.

31 Isaiah's call to prophesy is recorded in Isaiah 6.

32 For Isaiah's critique of Israel's corrupt religion and vision of international reconciliation, see Isaiah 1:10-25 and 19:23-25.

33 Heschel, *The Prophets*, 3-5.

34 Jesus states this explicitly in Matthew 5:43-48 and 7:9-12.

35 Dietrich Bonhoeffer, *Barcelona, Berlin, New York: 1928–1931*, edited by Clifford Green, translated by Douglas Stott (Minneapolis, MN: Fortress Press, 2008), 336.

Søren Kierkegaard developed this paradoxical vision of knowledge in his journal: "It is the duty of the human understanding to understand that there are things which it cannot understand and what those things are." See Robert Bretall (editor), *A Kierkegaard Anthology* (Princeton, NJ: Princeton University Press, 1946), 153.

Chapter 3
What Do You Want? Your Kingdom Come

1 W.H. Auden, "The Garrison" (August 1969), in W.H. *Auden: Collected Poems*, edited by Edward Mendelson (New York, NY: Random House, 1976), 633-634.

2 Bessel van der Kolk, *The Body Keeps the Score: Brain, Mind, and Body in the Healing of Trauma* (New York: Penguin Books, 2015), 17. For a profound study of newness and human imagination, see Michael North, *Novelty: A History of the New* (Chicago, IL: University of Chicago Press, 2013).

3 For sweeping interpretations of human history, see Yuval Harari, *Sapiens: A Brief History of Humankind* (New York, NY: HarperPerennial, 2018) and David Graeber and David Wengrow, *The Dawn of Everything: A New History of Humanity* (New York, NY: Farrar, Straus and Giroux, 2021).

4 See Donald Kraybill, *The Upside-Down Kingdom* (Harrisonburg, VA: Herald Press, 2018); Walter Brueggemann, *The Prophetic Imagination* (Minneapolis, MN: Fortress Press, 2001); and David Gushee and Glen Stassen, *Kingdom Ethics: Following Jesus in Contemporary Context* (Grand Rapids, MI: Eerdmans, 2017).

5 Jesus describes the unpredictable and uncontrollable nature of the kingdom in a late-night chat with a religious leader named Nicodemus in John 3:3-5.

6 Jesus describes the effects and precious value of the kingdom in Matthew 6:19-34; 13:44-45; Mark 9:47.

7 Jesus says this in Matthew 21:31-32.

8 James Baldwin, "A Talk to Teachers," in *James Baldwin: Collected Essays*, edited by Toni Morrison (New York, New York: The Library of America, 1998), 685.

9 These fifty unique references to the kingdom in Jesus's career include announcements, sayings, stories, teachings, and prayer. Space prevents me from discussing all of them in this chapter, but I believe these five signs accurately summarize them.

  It strikes me as important that Jesus never refers to humans "building" the kingdom. His invitation is in the tension of witness and work, passivity and activity. He teaches us to call for the kingdom to come and to desire God's will to be done. But he doesn't explicitly say that we humans bring the kingdom or make God's will happen. I believe Jesus maintains this tension, because he realizes how easily we imagine ourselves as the possessors of God, which leads to corruption, coercion, and harm.

10 On the moral imagination, see John Paul Lederach, *The Moral Imagination: The Art and Soul of Peacebuilding* (New York, NY: Oxford University Press, 2010).

11 Howard Thurman, *Jesus and the Disinherited* (Boston, MA: Beacon Press, 1996), 79.

12 Jesus tells this story in Matthew 25:31-46. For an extremely rich study of how Jesus's story has been interpreted across history, see Sherman Gray, *The Least of My Brothers: Matthew 25:31-46: A History of Interpretation* (Atlanta, GA: Scholars Press, 1989).

13 St. Augustine, *Homilies on the First Epistle of John, in The Works of Saint Augustine* I/14, translated by Boniface Ramsey (Hyde Park, NY: New City Press, 2008), 43.

14 When Jesus was dedicated as an infant at the Temple, his parents brought the smallest offering allowed for the poor who couldn't afford anything more (Luke 2:22-24; Leviticus 12:2-8). This indicates that Jesus was raised in an impoverished family. Jesus is then taken to Egypt as a refugee of political violence (Matthew 2:13-23).

15 For some examples and elaboration, see Matthew 11:19; 4:23-25; Mark 5:1-20; Luke 2:7; 9:58; 10:51-55.

16 See Matthew 24:14 and Luke 14:21-23. Mother Maria of Paris was a twice-divorced Russian woman who became a nun, resisted the Nazis, and rescued Jewish children from Hitler's death camps. Before she was murdered in a concentration camp, she declared, "At

the Last Judgment I shall not be asked whether I was successful in my ascetic exercises, nor how many bows and prostrations I made. Instead I shall be asked, Did I feed the hungry, clothe the naked, and visit the sick and prisoners? That is all I shall be asked." See *Mother Maria Skobtsova: Essential Writings* (Maryknoll, NY: Orbis Books, 2003).

17 Martin Luther King Jr., "Nonviolence and Racial Justice," in *A Testament of Hope: The Essential Writings and Speeches of Martin Luther King Jr.*, edited by James Washington (New York, NY: HarperOne, 1991), 9.

18 For Jesus's statements, see Matthew 5:3-12; 8:10-11; 24:14; Luke 14:10-14, 21-23.

19 Kendrick Lamar, "The Heart Part 5," promotional single for *Mr. Morale and the Big Steppers* (Interscope: 2022). See Matthew 20:25-28 and Luke 22:24-30.

20 For examples, see Matthew 4:23; 9:35; 10:7; 12:28.

21 See Matthew 12:28 and Luke 17:20-21.

22 For interpretations of Jesus's movement within his political context and ours today, see Richard Horsley, *Jesus and Empire: The Kingdom of God and the New World Disorder* (Minneapolis, MN: Fortress Press, 2002) and John Dominic Crossan, *God and Empire: Jesus Against Rome, Then and Now* (New York, NY: HarperOne, 2008).

23 See John 18:38; Luke 23:34, 42, 46; Matthew 27:46.

24 See Karl Marx, "Contribution to the Critique of Hegel's Philosophy of Right," in *The Marx-Engels Reader*, edited by Robert Tucker (New York, NY: W. W. Norton & Company, 1978), 54.

25 Thich Nhat Hanh, *Essential Writings* (Maryknoll, NY: Orbis Books, 2001), 141.

26 See Michael Nagler, *The Nonviolence Handbook: A Guide for Practical Action* (San Francisco, CA: Berrett-Koehler Publishers, 2014), 25, and David Hartsough and Joyce Hollyday, *Waging Peace: Adventures of a Lifelong Activist* (Oakland, CA: PM Press, 2014).

27 Martin Luther King Jr., "Facing the Challenge of a New Age," in *A Testament of Hope: The Essential Writings and Speeches of Martin Luther King Jr.*, edited by James Washington (New York, NY: HarperOne, 1991), 139.

28 W.H. Auden, "The Garrison" (August 1969), in *W.H. Auden: Collected Poems*, edited by Edward Mendelson (New York, NY: Random House, 1976), 633-634.

29 For an award-winning study of Christian racism, colonialism, and how to resist them, see Willie Jennings, *The Christian Imagination: Theology and the Origins of Race* (New Haven, CT: Yale University Press, 2011).

Chapter 4
How Much Is Enough? Our Daily Bread

1 Khalil Gibran, "On Buying and Selling," available online at poetryfoundation.org.

2 The source of this possibly apocryphal story is unknown to me. But for Rockefeller's story, see Ron Chernow, *Titan: The Life of John D. Rockefeller, Sr.* (New York, NY: Vintage, 2004).

3 Edward Burnays, a nephew of Sigmund Freud, was a founding architect of "public relations" and modern advertising. See the BBC documentary by Adam Curtis *Century of the Self* (2002). The first part is entitled "Happiness Machines."

4 The word that we translate as "daily" (*epiousion*) is a bit of a mystery. It's the only time the word appears in the Bible, and its meaning isn't certain. Early translations rendered it as "daily," and we'll follow this convention.

5 I share more of Wudenesh and Itash's story in my essays "You Are Precious: The Girl Who Taught Me Neighbor-Love," March 2, 2019 at andrew-decort.com and "Pilgrimage: A Transformative Model of Theological Education," on the University of Chicago's blog *The Craft of Teaching in the Academic Study of Religion*, March 5, 2018 at craftofteachingreligion.wordpress.com. I share their stories with their permission.

6 Unless otherwise noted, all translations from Hebrew scripture in this section use Robert Alter's *The Five Books of Moses: A Translation with Commentary* (New York, NY: W.W. Norton & Company, 2004).

7 Here I use *The Translation of the Jewish Study Bible* (New York, NY: Oxford University Press, 1999).

8 The notion that faith is a matter of "absolute dependence" on God was popularized by the German theologian, Friedrich Schleiermacher (1768-1834). See his *On Religion: Speeches to Its Cultured Despisers* (New York, NY: Cambridge University Press, 1996). The book on Schleiermacher that I have learned the most from is Matthew R. Robinson, *Redeeming Relationships, Relationships that Redeem: Free Sociability and the Completion of Humanity in the Thought of Friedrich Schleiermacher* (Tübingen: Mohr Siebeck, 2018).

9 I share more of Eyob's story and pictures of his life in my essay "Eyob: My Saint of Darkness," March 10, 2019 at andrew-decort.com.

10 For a profound and beautiful book on human and nonhuman empathy, see Frans de Waal, *The Age of Empathy: Nature's Lessons for a Kinder Society* (New York, NY: Crown, 2010).

11 "Companion" comes from the Latin roots *com-* "with" and *pan* "bread." The Ethiopian Amharic word for neighbor *balinjera* has the exact same meaning: someone with whom you are willing to share your bread (*injera*). This is why the Amharic name of the Neighbor-Love Movement is Balinjeraye or My Neighbor. It names our willingness to enter into relationships of mutual dignity and interdependence with others across boundaries. I tell the story of the Neighbor-Love Movement in chapter six.

12 In *Mass Starvation: The History and Future of Famine* (Cambridge, UK: Polity, 2017), Alex de Waal convincingly argues that modern famines are human-made, avoidable, and contingent on political failures or decisions that weaponize hunger. That is, hunger is not due to a shortage of food, but a shortage of human empathy, imagination, and action. Our 900,000 Ethiopian neighbors in famine are in my heart as I write this.

13 This practical program is described in the Book of Acts 6:1-3, the companion volume to the biographies of Jesus telling the story of his early movement.

The early Christian letter 1 Timothy 6:6-10 offers one of the most beautiful summaries of Jesus's challenging vision of enough: "But godliness with contentment is great gain. For we brought nothing into the world, and we can take nothing out of it. But if we have food and clothing, we will be content with that. Those who want to get rich fall into temptation and a trap and into many foolish and harmful desires that plunge people into ruin and destruction. For the love of money is a root of all kinds of evil. Some people, eager for money, have wandered from the faith and pierced themselves with many griefs."

14 For extensive documentation of this cultural revolution, see Gary Anderson, *Charity: The Place of the Poor in the Biblical Tradition* (New Haven, CT: Yale University Press, 2013); Helen Rhee, *Wealth and Poverty in Early Christianity* (Minneapolis, MN: Fortress Press, 2017); Peter Brown, *Through the Eye of a Needle: Wealth, the Fall of Rome, and the Making of Christianity in the West, 350-550 AD* (Princeton, NJ: Princeton University Press, 2012); and Ronald Sider, *Rich Christians in an Age of Hunger: Moving from Affluence to Generosity* (Nashville, TN: W Publishing Group, 2015).

15 For a holistic vision of development, see Bryant Myers, *Walking with the Poor: Principles and Practices of Transformational Development*, revised and expanded edition (Maryknoll, NY: Orbis, 2011).

Chapter 5
How Do We Begin Again? Forgive Us as We Forgive Others

1 James Baldwin, "Lockridge: 'The American Myth'" and "The Crusade of Indignation," in *James Baldwin: Collected Essays*, edited by Toni Morrison (New York, New York: The Library of America, 1998), 593 and 613.

2 Desmond Tutu, *An African Prayer Book* (New York, NY: Image, 1995), 38.

3 Jesus introduces his fifth movement of prayer with *kai*, a Greek conjunction indicating connection with what came before but also the introduction of something new. Richard Rohr writes about "the second half of life" in his book *Falling Upward: A Spirituality for the Two Halves of Life* (San Francisco, CA: Jossey-Bass, 2011). For Rohr, "the second half of life" names the new maturity that emerges in us when we grow beyond dualistic, us-versus-them mindsets and honestly face ourselves. In many ways, the second half of Jesus's prayer invites us into the spiritual practices we need for the second half of life.

4 Quoted in Stanley Cohen, *States of Denial: Knowing about Atrocities and Suffering* (Malden, MA: Polity Press, 2016), 24-25. I'm grateful to James Hoey for introducing me to Bollas's insight and this book.

5 Amanda Gorman, *Poems: Call Us What We Carry* (New York, NY: Viking, 2021), 57.

6 Matthew's version says, "Forgive us our debts as we forgive our debtors." Luke's version says, "Forgive us our sins, for we also forgive everyone who is indebted to us." Whether Jesus refers to "sins" or "debts," the idea is the same: we have failure and unfinished business that needs to be resolved. Forgiving debts had profound economic and political implications in Jesus's context and ours today. See Peter Hertig, "The Jubilee Mission of Jesus in the Gospel of Luke: Reversals of Fortune," *Missiology: An International Review*, April 1, 1998.

7 Amanda Gorman, *Poems: Call Us What We Carry*, 83.

8 Jesus was the first person in history to so profoundly understand and prioritize forgiveness. He teaches on it at least ten times in our surviving records, making forgiveness one of his central topics. See Hannah Arendt, *The Human Condition*, second edition (Chicago, IL: University of Chicago Press, 1998), 215.

9 See Arthur Brooks, *Love Your Enemies: How Decent People Can Save America from the Culture of Contempt* (New York, NY: Broadside Books, 2019), 34-36.

10 Bessel van der Kolk, *The Body Keeps the Score: Brain, Mind, and Body in the Healing of Trauma* (New York: Penguin Books, 2015), 354.

11 Curt Thompson, *The Anatomy of the Soul* (Carol Stream, IL: Tyndale Momentum, 2010), 233. See James 5:14-16 where the author traditionally identified as Jesus's brother connects confession, forgiveness, and healing.

12 For similar visions of forgiveness, see Desmond Tutu, *No Future Without Forgiveness* (New York, NY: Doubleday, 1999), 270-272; Martin Luther King Jr., *Strength to Love* (Minneapolis, MN: Fortress Press, 2010), 44-45; and bell hooks, *All About Love: New Visions* (New York, NY: William Morrow, 2001), 138-139.

13 bell hooks, *All About Love*, xxviii.

14 David Livingstone Smith, *On Inhumanity: Dehumanization and How to Resist It* (New York, NY: Oxford University Press, 2021), 6.

15 For important studies on "othering" or how we come to see others as unrelated or less than ourselves, see Toni Morrison, *The Origin of Others* (Cambridge, MA: Harvard University Press, 2017); Sam Keen, *Faces of the Enemy: Reflections of the Hostile Imagination* (New York, NY: Harper & Row, 1986); and David Livingstone Smith, *Less than Human: Why We Demean, Enslave, and Exterminate Others* (New York, NY: St. Martin's Press, 2011).

16 Nelson Mandela, *Long Walk to Freedom: The Autobiography of Nelson Mandela* (New York, NY: Bayback Books, 1994), 176.

17 Desmond Tutu, *No Future Without Forgiveness* (New York, NY: Doubleday, 1999), 165.

18 Jesus expressed extraordinary generosity and trust in the power of forgiveness. He said, "Anyone who speaks a word against the Son of Humanity [himself] will be forgiven" (Matthew 12:32). He refused to allow insults and rejections to become the basis of permanent separation from others.

19 Desmond Tutu, *An African Prayer Book* (New York, NY: Image, 1995), 38, xviii.

20 Howard Thurman, *Jesus and the Disinherited* (Boston, MA: Beacon Press, 1996), 62.

21 See "Birkat Ha-Minim" on the *Jewish Virtual Library* website at jewishvirtuallibrary.org.

22 Jesus unpacks these countercultural practices of nonviolent resistance in Matthew 5:38-45 and Luke 6:27-31.

23 Nelson Mandela, *Long Walk to Freedom: The Autobiography of Nelson Mandela* (New York, NY: Bayback Books, 1994), 192, 201, 387, 568.

24 Denis Mukwege, *The Power of Women: A Doctor's Journey of Hope and Healing* (New York, NY: Flatiron Books, 2021), 192.

25 Amanda Gorman, *Poems: Call Us What We Carry* (New York, NY: Viking, 2021), 43.

26 Dr. Mukwege unpacks this deadly economy in *The Power of Women*, 113-120.

27 Dr. Denis Mukwege, "Nobel Lecture," December 10, 2018 at nobelprize.org.

28 Bessel van der Kolk, *The Body Keeps the Score: Brain, Mind, and Body in the Healing of Trauma* (New York: Penguin Books, 2015), 54-55. See also Mark Wolynn, *It Didn't Start with You: How Inherited Family Trauma Shapes Who We Are and How to End the Cycle* (New York, NY: Penguin Books, 2017).

29 Elizabeth Kübler-Ross and David Kessler, *On Grief and Grieving: Finding the Meaning of Grief Through the Five Stages of Loss* (New York, NY: Scribner, 2005), xiii.

30 David Livingstone Smith, *On Inhumanity: Dehumanization and How to Resist It* (New York, NY: Oxford University Press, 2021), 187.

31 Polish Jews suffered horrifically, often being targeted by Germans and their Polish neighbors. For a devastating account of this violence, see Jan T. Gross, *Neighbors: The Destruction of the Jewish Community in Jedwabne, Poland* (New York, NY: Penguin Books, 2002).

32 Quoted in Jim Forest, *Loving Our Enemies: Reflections on the Hardest Commandment* (Maryknoll, NY: Orbis Books, 2014), 118-119.

33 I recommend two documentaries about forgiveness in response to extraordinary hatred, violence, and trauma. *As We Forgive* (2008) directed by Laura Waters Hinson explores the Rwandan genocide and how women survivors chose to forgive the killers of their families. *Emanuel* (2019) directed by Brian Ivie explores the racist massacre at Mother Emanuel Church in Charleston, South Carolina and how African American survivors chose to forgive the perpetrator Dylann Roof. These documentaries powerfully challenge the view that forgiveness is weak and enables further injustice.

34 Jesus goes on to say, "If you don't forgive them, they are not forgiven." Jesus has just risen from the dead after forgiving his killers, so it's unlikely that Jesus is suggesting that we should dangle forgiveness in front of others and then withhold it. It seems that Jesus is naming the sobering reality of what's at stake: when we don't forgive, our relationships remain broken and our new beginning is cut off.

Chapter 6
Can Violence Save Us? Deliver Us from Evil

1 Kendrick Lamar, "The Heart Part 5," on Mr. Morale & the Big Steppers (Interscope, 2022).

2 Mohandas Gandhi, *The Collected Works of Mahatma Gandhi, Volume 72: April 16 – September 11, 1940* (New Delhi: The Publications Division, 1978), 416 and *The Collected Works of Mahatma Gandhi, Volume 82: November 1, 1945 – January 19, 1946* (New Delhi: The Publications Division, 1980), 67. I'm grateful to Professor Wolfgang Palaver for these quotations. I'm aware that Gandhi made racist statements,

which his own values rightly condemn.

3 Peter Maas, *Love Thy Neighbor: A Story of War* (New York, NY: Knopf Doubleday, 1997), 15.

4 "Good trouble" is a phrase borrowed from the Civil Rights activist and Congressperson John Lewis (1940-2020).

5 The Greek word translated here as "temptation" is *peirasmon*. It can mean temptation, test, or trial. It taps into the Hebrew prophets' vision of our lives and histories building toward decisive turning points that surge with the agony of childbirth. The outcome can be destruction and grief, or new life and joy. Jesus is inviting us to anticipate these crucial moments and to premeditate the delivering presence of God in them.

6 To learn more about the Neighbor-Love Movement, our covenant, and seven practices, visit nlmglobal.org.

7 David Livingstone Smith, *On Inhumanity: Dehumanization and How to Resist It* (New York, NY: Oxford University Press, 2021), 187, 6.

8 See Andrew DeCort, "Christian Nationalism Is Tearing Ethiopia Apart," *Foreign Policy*, June 18, 2022 at foreignpolicy.com and Jeffrey York, "Tigray Has Seen Up to Half a Million Dead from Violence and Starvation," *Globe & Mail*, March 14, 2022 at theglobeandmail.com.

9 See Genocide Watch's country profile for Ethiopia at genocidewatch.com.

10 My early interviews with Eskinder Nega were published by the *Public Theology Network*. See Andrew DeCort, "From Prison to Public Theology in Ethiopia, Parts I and II," *Public Theology Network* on June 4 and June 11, 2018 at politicaltheology.com.

11 My interviews with Jawar are published on my Facebook page entitled "Interview with Jawar Mohammed: Childhood, Faith, Ethics, Society" on May 5, 2021 at facebook.com.

12 Thankfully, both were released after eighteen months in prison on these unsubstantiated charges. I remain in regular conversation with Jawar. Eskinder hasn't responded to my messages.

13 For a classic study of the "mimetic" or imitative nature of violence, see Rene Girard, *Saw Satan Fall Like Lightning* (Maryknoll, NY: Orbis, 2001).

14 Interpreting "temptation" as high-stress, flight-or-fight situations that trigger us to unleash more evil may be unfamiliar to some readers. Contemporary Christian usage often sees "temptation" as the desire to do naughty little things: steal a candy bar, have a dance floor makeout, deface a building. But the twenty-one references to temptation in the New Testament have a fiercer meaning. They focus on our distress, greed, conflict, and the suffering that comes from violence. Think of these two familiar passages in the life of Peter.

First, after Peter's failed temptation and Jesus's resurrection, Jesus personally restores Peter by asking him the same question three times in a row: "Peter, do you love me? Then feed my sheep." It seems that Jesus is asking Peter if he still loves and trusts who Jesus is after Peter felt betrayed by Jesus's nonviolent death. And so Jesus calls him to gently nurture his "sheep," vulnerable creatures that are often destined for slaughter.

Notice that Jesus warns Peter to get ready to surrender his freedom and be killed for this way of life. Jesus's final word to Peter is, "Follow me" — or *keep practicing* (see John 21:15-22).

Second, Peter himself later associates "temptation" with violent conflict and suffering. Similar to Jesus, he advises his community, "Commit yourselves to your faithful Creator and continue to do good" (1 Peter 1:3-9; 5:12-19). Paul, a converted religious extremist, also uses the term "temptation" in a context of violence and suffering. He says that he endured this "with great humility and with tears" — essentially Jesus's response as we'll see below (Acts 20:19).

In short, Peter's temptation was his religious nationalism and trust in violence for salvation amidst life-threatening conflict under Rome's brutal empire.

15 Howard Thurman, *Jesus and the Disinherited* (Boston, MA: Beacon Press, 1996), 46.

16 Thich Nhat Hanh, *Essential Writings* (Maryknoll, NY: Orbis Books, 2001), 132.

17 See Matthew 26:35; Mark 14:31; Luke 22:33; John 13:37. In Luke 22:36-38, Jesus warns his disciples and says, "If you don't have a sword, sell your cloak and buy one." Jesus is clearly using hyperbole to warn them about the coming danger — not calling them to arm themselves for violence. First, Jesus had just taught them not to copy the domineering pattern of "lording over others" (Luke 22:25-27). Second, when the disciples say they have "two swords," Jesus answers, "That's enough!" — clearly not enough for violent resistance (Luke 22:38). Ron Sider provides a compelling discussion in his book *If Jesus Is Lord: Loving Our Enemies in an Age of Violence* (Grand Rapids, MI: Baker Academic, 2019).

18 For groundbreaking studies of the Christian version of religious nationalism today, see Andrew Whitehead and Samuel Perry, *Taking America Back for God: Christian Nationalism in the United States* (New York, NY: Oxford University Press, 2020) and Kristin Kobes du Mez, *Jesus and John Wayne: How Evangelicals Corrupted a Faith and Fractured a Nation* (New York, NY: Liveright, 2020).

19 Howard Thurman, *Jesus and the Disinherited* (Boston, MA: Beacon Press, 1996), 59.

20 See Peter Coleman, "Half the U.S. Believes Another Civil War is Likely. Here Are the 5 Steps We Must Take to Avoid that," *Time Magazine*, January 6, 2022, at time.com. Coleman writes, "Neuroscience research has found that our more central attitudes and opinions often come to be embodied in neural structures in our brains... movement has been found to be particularly conducive to increasing key aspects of good conflict engagement, like creativity, flexibility and positivity." See also Bessel van der Kolk, "Befriending the Body," in *The Body Keeps the Score* (New York, NY: Penguin, 2014), 102-103 and Christine Webb, Maya Rossignac-Milon, and E. Tory Higgins, "Stepping Forward Together: Could Walking Facilitate Interpersonal Conflict Resolution?" in *The American Psychologist*, May-June 2017; 72(4):373-385 at pubmed.ncbi.nlm.nih.gov.

21 Elizabeth Kübler-Ross and David Kessler, *On Grief and Grieving: Finding the Meaning of Grief Through the Five Stages of Loss* (New York, NY: Scribner, 2005), 63.

22 Carl Rogers, *On Becoming a Person: A Therapist's View of Psychotherapy* (New York, NY: HarperOne, 1995), 151. For a beautiful study integrating spirituality, neuroscience, and human transformation, see Gena St. David, *The Brain and the*

Body: Unlocking the Transformative Potential of the Story of Christ (Eugene, OR: Cascade Books, 2021).

23 Here in the face of suffering, Jesus hears the voice from heaven say, "I have glorified your name and will glorify it again" (John 12:28). Strikingly, the word "glorify" shares the same root as "I delight in you," echoing God's first and repeated message to Jesus.

24 Mohandas Gandhi, *The Collected Works of Mahatma Gandhi, Volume 72: April 16 – September 11, 1940* (New Delhi: The Publications Division, 1978), 416.

25 Howard Thurman, *Jesus and the Disinherited* (Boston, MA: Beacon Press, 1996), 91.

26 Neuroscience research has explored the intersection of stress, falling asleep, and vulnerability to aggressive behavior. See Laura Grace and Seema Bhatnagar, "Orexins and Stress," in *Frontiers in Neuroendocrinology*, 2018 October; 51:132-145.

27 See Matthew 26:56 and Luke 22:62. Interpreters often assume that Peter denied Jesus three times because he was afraid of being associated with a man who was arrested and about to be executed. But Peter is obviously not a coward or afraid of death. In fact, Peter has just proven that he's ready to kill and be killed for Jesus, just like he promised (Matthew 26:35).

Making sense of Peter's betrayal requires a more subtle interpretation. Peter himself must have felt bitterly betrayed by Jesus. Surging with adrenaline, Peter had just exercised the most heroic, ultimate form of human loyalty: violence. And then Jesus immediately responded by undoing Peter's violently loyal act, healing his victim, and publicly condemning Peter's behavior.

More likely, then, Peter repeatedly denied knowing Jesus because he felt betrayed and disappointed by Jesus. When the chips were down and the critical moment arrived—the much anticipated "temptation" or "trial"—Peter thought that it was *Jesus* who had crumbled by refusing to fight back and unleash a violent messianic movement to liberate Israel and take power by force. It seems Peter was outraged and couldn't tolerate associating himself with this failed messiah who even healed the enemy. Peter's religious nationalism and trust in violence betrayed a real knowledge of Jesus and willingness to practice with him.

28 Martin Luther King Jr., *A Testament of Hope: The Essential Writings and Speeches of Martin Luther King Jr.*, edited by James Washington (New York, NY: HarperOne, 1991), 349.

Tertullian (155-220 AD), one of the earliest African interpreters of Jesus, says that Jesus here "unbelts" Peter and "disarms every soldier." Quoted in David Gushee, *The Sacredness of Human Life: Why an Ancient Biblical Vision Is Key to the World's Future* (Grand Rapids, MI: Eerdmans, 2013), 123.

29 See Luke 23:2; John 19:10 and 20:36-37.

30 For examples of Liukin's stunning landings, see "Anastasia Liukin Sticking the Landing for Two Minutes Straight" on GymnasticsEverywhere (YouTube channel).

31 Liukin's quote appears in numerous places online, but I haven't found a definitive published source.

32 Howard Thurman, *Jesus and the Disinherited* (Boston, MA: Beacon Press, 1996), 83. With defiant irony, Jesus said that his execution would really be his enthronement—the moment when his divine belovedness would be on full display and undeniable (John 8:28). Jesus's nonviolent death is the inversion and abolition of religious terrorism: God is embodied and revealed through self-giving love—not through other-destroying violence (Luke 21:34-36). The Gospels record that at least one of Jesus's executioners had a conversion experience as he watched Jesus die. He confessed, "This man was truly the Son of God" (Matthew 27:54; Mark 15:39).

33 Amanda Gorman, *Poems: Call Us What We Carry* (New York, NY: Viking, 2021), 55.

34 N.T. Wright, *The Lord and His Prayer* (Grand Rapids, MI: Eerdmans, 1996), 76.

35 I explore the process of transforming rather than transmitting pain in my essay "Pain, Intimacy, and Neighbor-Love," *Pace Journal*, Vol. 2 (Singapore: Pace, 2022).

36 John Dear, *The Beatitudes of Peace: Meditations on the Beatitudes, Peacemaking, and the Spiritual Life* (New London, CT: Twenty-Third Publications, 2016), 108.

37 I want to emphasize that forgiveness is a *process*. It takes time and patience and must be practiced. After I was rejected by Christian leaders that I deeply cared about, I practiced saying a blessing over them each time they entered my mind. I didn't deny the pain of what they did, but this was my way of practicing toward forgiveness and healing. I continue this practice today over ten years later.

Chapter 7
Can You Let Go of Power and Prestige? Yours Forever

1 Niccolo Machiavelli, *The Prince: A Revised Translation, Backgrounds, Interpretations, Marginalia*, edited by Robert M. Adams (New York: W. W. Norton & Company, 1992), 11.

2 Julian of Norwich, *Revelations of Divine Love*, translated by Barry Windeatt (New York, NY: Oxford University Press, 2015), 22.

3 Johnny Cash, "Hurt," track 3 on *American IV: The Man Comes Around* (Universal, 2002). This song was originally written by Nine Inch Nails.

4 I'm reminded of Eyob here. Eyob was only 13 years-old, but he had the maturity of an elder who had lived with mindfulness for a lifetime. He was full of hope, and he was ready to let go with trust in our Father.

5 We don't know with certainty if this last movement was originally in Jesus's prayer or not. Some ancient manuscripts include it, others don't. This is why some translations of the Bible include this line, while others exclude it or put it in a footnote. Whether this conclusion is original to Jesus or not, it powerfully summarizes the spirit of his prayer and spirituality: trust and surrender to God. As we'll see, it also brilliantly reverses the satanic temptation, "All this will be yours," which roots it in Jesus's biography.

6 See Jim Collins, *Good to Great: Why Some Companies Make the Leap and Others Don't* (New York, NY: Harper Business, 2001) and Umair Haque, "The Great to Good Manifesto," *Harvard Business Review*, February 3, 2010.

7   See Friedrich Nietzsche, *Beyond Good and Evil*, edited by Rolf-Peter Horstmann and Judy Norman, translated by Judith Norman (New York, NY: Cambridge University Press, 2005), I, §9 and §259.

8   For a wonderful book on the positive possibilities of our brain chemistry, see Paul Zak, *The Moral Molecule: How Trust Works* (New York, NY: Plume, 2013).

9   Daniel Silliman, "The Christian Peacemaker Who Left a Trail of Trauma," *Christianity Today*, November 26, 2021 at christianitytoday.com.

10 Curt Thompson, *The Soul of Shame: Retelling Our Stories We Believe about Ourselves* (Downers Grove, IL: IVP Books, 2015), 48 and 22.

11 See John 5:41 and 8:50 where Jesus rejects glory; Luke 18:18-25 where Jesus calls the rich man to give away everything to the poor; and Matthew 16:20 where Jesus commands his disciples to keep his movement secret. There are many other examples of all three.

12 See Luke 24:26; John 11:4, 40; 17:4-5.

13 For a scholarly study of Jesus's resurrection, I recommend N.T. Wright, *The Resurrection of the Son of God* (Minneapolis, MN: Fortress Press, 2003). For a popular discussion of resurrection hope, see N.T. Wright, *Surprised by Hope: Rethinking Heaven, the Resurrection, and the Mission of the Church* (New York, NY: Harper, 2008).

14 I borrow this pregnant line from Robert Bellah's gigantic and brilliant tome *Religion in Human Evolution: From the Paleolithic to the Axial Age* (Cambridge, MA: Belknap Harvard University Press, 2011).

15 In chapter one, I touched on this profound distinction that Jesus makes between "destruction" and "death." We will all die, but we will not all be destroyed. See Luke 21:17-19.

16 See Matthew 28:16-20; Luke 24:36-49; John 20:19-31; 21:15-35.

17 Polycarp (69-155 AD) was the first Christian martyr. Justyn Martyr (100-165 AD) was the first Christian philosopher and also a martyr. Both were condemned to death as atheists. See Justin Martyr, *First Apology in The Ante-Nicene Fathers: Translations of the Writings of the Fathers down to A.D. 325*, Vol. 1, edited by Alexander Roberts and James Donaldson (New York, NY: Scribner's Sons, 1905), 165, and *The Martyrdom of Polycarp*, III.2 and XIII.2 in *The Apostolic Fathers*, Vol. II, translated by Kirsopp Lake, Loeb Classical Library (New York, NY: The Macmillan Co., 1923), 317 and 329.

18 Some may question whether the early Jesus movement was truly "multi-gender." As I mentioned in chapter one, the Christian movement has struggled to accept and integrate Jesus's rejection of patriarchy for an unprecedented egality. But women were crucial leaders in the early centuries of Jesus's movement. For a comprehensive study of the evidence, see Lynn Cohick and Amy Brown Hughs, *Christian Women in the Patristic World: Their Influence, Authority, and Legacy in the Second Through Fifth Centuries* (Grand Rapids, MI: Baker Academic, 2017).

19 The Roman Empire tried to colonize Jesus's movement. This began under Emperor Constantine "the Great" (272-337 AD) with his imperial Edict of Milan in 313 AD. That imperial colonization continues today in various places and forms. But the

corruption of Christianity doesn't falsify Jesus's movement or exhaust its possibility. David Gushee's *The Sacredness of Human Life: Why an Ancient Biblical Vision Is Key to the World's Future* (Grand Rapids, MI: Eerdmans, 2013) helpfully unpacks the core values of Jesus's movement, how it was corrupted under Constantine, and how it continues today.

See also Rodney Stark, *The Rise of Christianity: How the Obscure, Marginal Jesus Movement Became the Dominant Religious Force in the Western World in a Few Centuries* (San Francisco, CA: Harper, 1997).

20 Private correspondence with Peter Hartwig on May 4, 2022. Peter edited *Flourishing on the Edge of Faith*, and I express my thanks for him and his brilliant work in the Gratitude section.

21 This is the story of *Star Wars: Episode IV—A New Hope* (1977) directed by George Lucas.

22 J.R.R. Tolkien, *The Fellowship of the Ring* (New York, NY: William Morrow, 2012), 63, 73.

23 J.R.R. Tolkien, *The Return of the King* (New York, NY: William Morrow, 2012). Chapter 3 "Mount Doom."

24 J.K. Rowling, *Harry Potter and the Sorcerer's Stone* (New York, NY: Scholastic, 1999), 291.

25 J.K. Rowling, *Harry Potter and the Deathly Hallows* (New York, NY: Scholastic, 2009), 242.

26 J.K. Rowling, *Harry Potter and the Goblet of Fire* (New York, NY: Scholastic, 2000), 648 and *Harry Potter and the Order of the Phoenix* (New York, NY: Scholastic, 2004), 814.

27 Rowling, *Deathly Hallows*, 434.

28 Rowling, *Deathly Hallows*, 563.

29 Rowling, *Deathly Hallows*, 708.

30 Rowling, *Deathly Hallows*, 710, 716, 722.

31 Rowling, *Deathly Hallows*, 741-742, 744.

32 See Rowling, *Deathly Hallows*, 748-749. This is how the movie version ends. In the book, Harry buries the wand in Dumbledore's tomb. Either way, the meaning is the same: Harry has abandoned the wand, and its power is broken.

33 Rowling, *Death Hallows*, 759.

34 Julian of Norwich, *Revelations of Divine Love*, translated by Barry Windeatt (New York, NY: Oxford University Press, 2015), 22.

35 I offer a more detailed interpretation of the *Harry Potter* story in my essay "The Ethics of Harry Potter," March 28, 2022 at andrew-decort.com.

Conclusion
A Billion Revolutions

1 James Baldwin, "White Racism or World Community?" in *James Baldwin: Collected Essays* (New York, NY: Library of America, 1998), 750.

Gratitude

1 Thomas Merton, letter to Abdul Aziz on April 4, 1962, in *A Life in Letters: The Essential Collection*, edited by William Shannon and Christine Bochen (New York, NY: HarperOne, 2008), 345.

BitterSweetCollective

BitterSweet Collective is a community-owned media house—a community of creatives collaborating together to produce stories, films, books, and other created works that orient us toward hope and challenge us to reject cynicism, defy apathy, and celebrate good. *Flourishing on the Edge of Faith* is our first book and Andrew DeCort is our first author, though we've been publishing shorter-form stories on many topics with many writers, photographers, and filmmakers for more than a decade: bittersweetmonthly.com.

The publishing of this book with our dear friend and respected scholar, Andrew, represents a monumental collaborative achievement for the BitterSweet team. Special and specific thanks to each contributor for their trust and investments of heart, soul, mind, and strength: Andrew DeCort, Peter Hartwig, Lori Parkerson, Obiekwe Okolo, Dave Baker, Sarah O'Malley, Holly Harris, Robert Winship, Greg Sitzmann, Steve Jeter, and Kate Schmidgall. There is much more to come and much more to be done, together.

For more information about BitterSweet Collective, visit bittersweetcollective.com

www.ingramcontent.com/pod-product-compliance
Lightning Source LLC
Chambersburg PA
CBHW011220120626
46545CB00010B/3088